Edexcel
GCSE MODULAR MATHEMATICS
Examples and Practice

HIGHER

Stage 3

1	Equations	1
2	Powers, proportion and calculator methods	14
3	Straight line and transformed graphs	25
4	Trigonometric functions	37
5	Circle theorems	48
6	Advanced measure and mensuration	57
7	Handling data	67
	Terminal practice paper 1	84
	Terminal practice paper 2	87
	Answers	91

Heinemann

Edexcel
Success through qualifications

About this book

This *Examples and Practice* book is designed to help you get the best possible grade in your Edexcel GCSE maths examination. The authors are senior examiners and coursework moderators and have a good understanding of Edexcel's requirements.

Higher Stage 3 Examples and Practice covers all the topics that will be tested in your Higher Stage 3 examination. You can use this book to revise, or you can use it throughout the course, alongside the *Edexcel GCSE Maths* Higher core textbook.

References in the contents list for each section of the book tell you when to find the most relevant paragraph of the specification. For example, NA2a refers to Number and Algebra, paragraph 2, section a.

Helping you prepare for your exam

To help you prepare, each topic offers:
- **Key points** to reinforce the key teaching concepts
- **Teaching references** showing you where the relevant material is covered in both the old and new editions of the *Edexcel GCSE Maths* Higher core textbook. These references show you where to find full explanations of concepts, and additional worked examples e.g.

> Teaching reference:
> *(pp 47–49, section 3.1, 3.2)* ── The first reference is to the old edition
> pp 53–56, section 3.2, 3.3 ── The second reference is to the new edition

Where material is new to the specification there is no reference to the old edition textbooks.
- **Worked examples** showing you how to tackle a problem and lay out your answer
- **Exercises** with references showing you which exercises in the *Edexcel GCSE Maths* Higher core textbook contain similar questions. The first reference, in brackets and italic, is to the old edition. The second reference is to the new edition.
- **A summary of key points** so you can check that you have covered all the key concepts

Which edition am I using?

The new editions of the *Edexcel GCSE Maths* core textbooks have yellow cover flashes saying 'ideal for the 2001 specification'. You can also use the old edition (no yellow cover flash) to help you prepare for your Stage 3 exam.

Exam practice and using the answers

An exam style practice paper at the back of the book will help you make sure that you are totally exam-ready. This paper is exactly the same length and standard as your actual Stage 3 exam.

Answers to all the questions are provided at the back of the book. Once you have completed an exercise you can use the answers to check whether you have made any mistakes. You need to show full working in your exam – it isn't enough to write down the answer.

The terminal papers

The terminal exam papers cover the full range of content given in the specification for all of Stage 3 in each tier. However, you may expect about half of the questions to be on Stage 3 content.

Contents

1 Equations
1.1	The intersection of a line and a parabola	NA5l, NA6c	1
1.2	The intersection of a line and a circle	NA5l, NA6c, NA6h	7

2 Powers, proportion and calculator methods
2.1	Powers and indices	Na3a	14
2.2	Surds	NA3n	16
2.3	Proportion	NA5h	18
2.4	Efficient and effective use of a calculator	NA3o	20

3 Straight line and transformed graphs
3.1	Straight line graphs	NA6c	25
3.2	Applying transformations to graphs	NA6g	27

4 Trigonometric functions
4.1	The sine rule	S2g	37
4.2	The cosine rule	S2g	38
4.3	Graphs of trigonometric functions	S2g	41
4.4	Solving simple trigonometric equations	S2g	43
4.5	Angles between a line and a plane	S2g	43

5 Circle theorems
5.1	Angles at the centre and circumference	S2h	48
5.2	Cyclic quadrilaterals	S2h	49
5.3	The alternate segment theorem	S2h	51
5.4	Geometrical proof	S2h	53

6 Advanced measure and mensuration
6.1	Dimension theory	S2f	57
6.2	3-D Pythagoras	S2f	58
6.3	Area of a segment	S3d	60
6.4	Area and volume of similar shapes	S2i, S3d	61
6.5	Compound solids	S2i	62

7 Handling data
7.1	Sampling	H2d	67
7.2	Grouped data 1 *freq. polygons*	H2d	70
7.3	Grouped data 2: histograms	H2d, H4a, H5d	73
7.4	Probability	H4d, H5g	76

Terminal practice paper 1	84
Terminal practice paper 2	87
Answers	91

Heinemann Educational Publishers,
Halley Court, Jordan Hill, Oxford, OX2 8EJ
a division of Reed Educational & Professional Publishing Ltd
Heinemann is a registered trademark of Reed Educational & Professional Publishing Ltd

OXFORD   MELBOURNE   AUCKLAND
JOHANNESBURG   BLANTYRE   GABORONE
IBADAN   PORTSMOUTH NH (USA)   CHICAGO

© Heinemann Educational Publishers

All rights reserved. No part of this publication may be reproduced, stored in a retrieval system, or transmitted in any form or by any means, electronic, mechanical, photocopying, recording, or otherwise without either the prior written permission of the Publishers or a licence permitting restricted copying in the United Kingdom issued by the Copyright Licensing Agency Ltd, 90 Tottenham Court Road, London W1P 1LP.

First published 2002

ISBN 0 435 53554 4

06 05 04 03 02
10 9 8 7 6 5 4 3 2 1

Designed and typeset by Tech-Set Ltd, Gateshead, Tyne and Wear
Cover photo: Stone Picture Library
Cover design by Miller, Craig and Cocking
Printed in the United Kingdom by Scotprint

Acknowledgements
The publishers and authors would like to thank Jean Linsky for her contribution and assistance with the manuscript.

The answers are not the responsibility of Edexcel.

Publishing team	**Design**	**Production**	**Author team**
Editorial	Phil Richards	David Lawrence	Karen Hughes
Sue Bennett	Colette Jacquelin	Jason Wyatt	Trevor Johnson
Lauren Bourque			Peter Jolly
Des Brady			David Kent
Nicholas Georgiou			Keith Pledger
Derek Huby			
Maggie Rumble			
Nick Sample			
Harry Smith			

Tel: 01865 888058   www.heinemann.co.uk

1 Equations

1.1 The intersection of a line and a parabola

- You can find the coordinates of the points of intersection of a line and a parabola graphically.
- You can solve a linear equation and a quadratic equation simultaneously by drawing the graphs for the equations. Their points of intersection represent the common solutions.

A parabola is the graph of a quadratic function.

Example 1
(a) Find graphically the coordinates of the points of intersection of the line with equation $y = x + 4$ and the parabola with equation $y = x^2 - 2$. Take values of x from -4 to 4.
(b) Use your answer to part (a) to solve the simultaneous equations $y = x + 4$ and $y = x^2 - 2$.

(a) Plot three points for $y = x + 4$, e.g. $(0, 4)$, $(1, 5)$ and $(2, 6)$.
Make a table of values for $y = x^2 - 2$:

x	-4	-3	-2	-1	0	1	2	3	4
y	14	7	2	-1	-2	-1	2	7	14

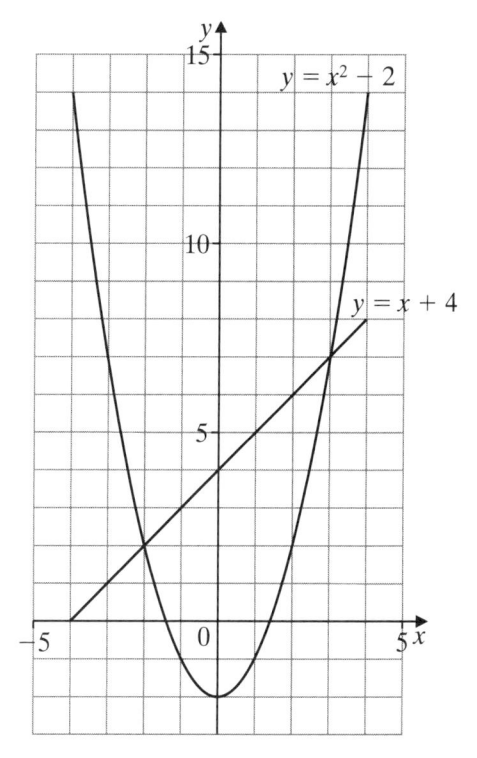

From the diagram, the coordinates of the points of intersection are $(-2, 2)$ and $(3, 7)$.

2 Equations

(b) The points of intersection represent the solutions of the simultaneous equations $y = x + 4$ and $y = x^2 - 2$. So the solutions are $x = -2, y = 2$ and $x = 3, y = 7$.

The x-coordinates of the points of intersection give the solutions of the quadratic equation $x^2 - 2 = x + 4$, which simplifies to $x^2 - x - 6 = 0$.

- **You can solve a quadratic equation by finding the x-coordinates of the points of intersection of a parabola and a straight line.**

Example 2
(a) Draw the graph of $y = x^2 + 2x - 1$. Take values of x from -4 to 4.
(b) By drawing a suitable straight line, use your graph to solve the quadratic equation $x^2 - x - 3 = 0$.
Give your answers correct to 1 decimal place.

(a) Make a table of values for $y = x^2 + 2x - 1$:

x	-4	-3	-2	-1	0	1	2	3	4
y	7	2	-1	-2	-1	2	7	14	23

Graph is drawn below.

(b) Write $x^2 - x - 3 = 0$ as $x^2 + 2x - 1 = 3x + 2$.
Then plot 3 points for the line with equation $y = 3x + 2$, e.g. $(0, 2)$, $(1, 5)$ and $(2, 8)$, and draw the line.

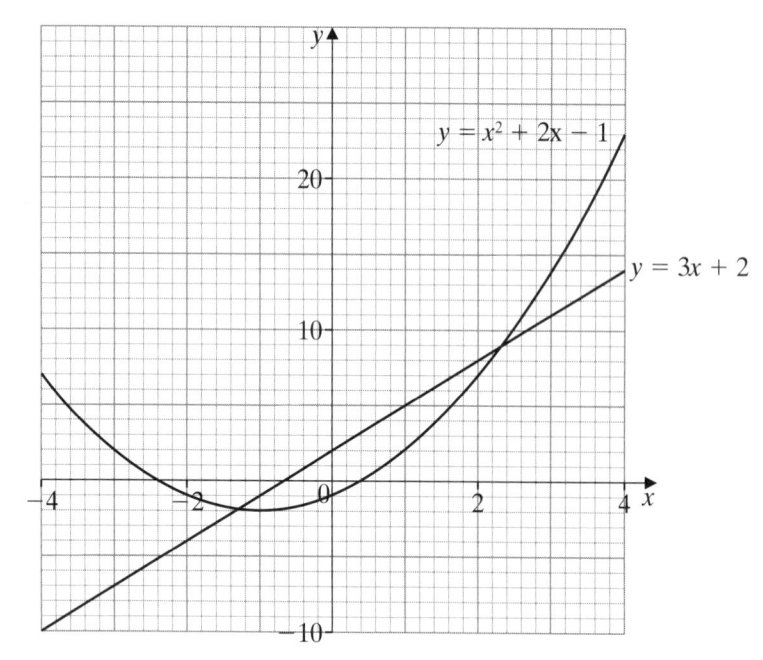

The x-coordinates of the points of intersection give the solutions to the quadratic equation $x^2 - x - 3 = 0$.
From the diagram, the solutions are $x = 2.3$ or $x = -1.3$.

Example 3

Solve graphically the simultaneous equations $x + y = 8$ and $y = 10 - x^2$.
Use values of x from -4 to 4.

Plot three points for $x + y = 8$, e.g. $(0, 8)$, $(2, 6)$ and $(4, 4)$.
Make a table of values for $y = 10 - x^2$:

x	-4	-3	-2	-1	0	1	2	3	4
y	-6	1	6	9	10	9	6	1	-6

From the graph, the solutions are

$x = -1, y = 9$ and $x = 2, y = 6$.

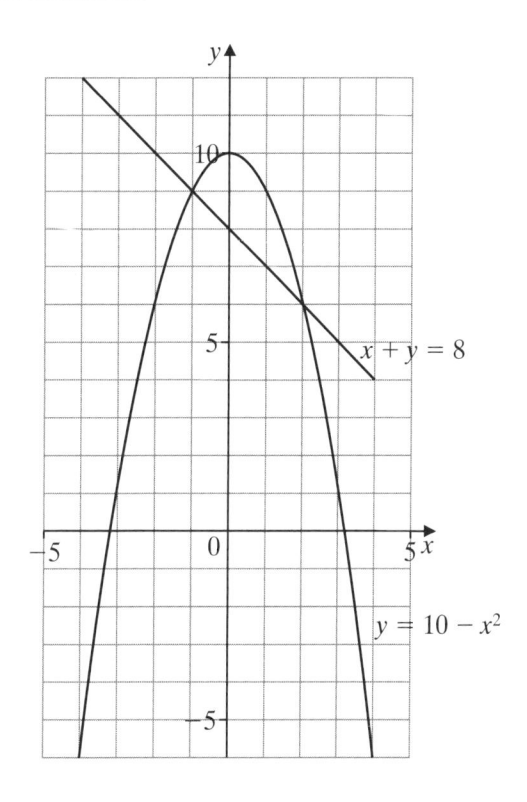

Exercise 1A

1 Find graphically the coordinates of the points of intersection of these parabolas and lines. Take values of x from -4 to 4.
   (a) $y = x^2$ and $y = x + 2$
   (b) $y = x^2$ and $y = 4x - 3$
   (c) $y = x^2 + 4$ and $y = 1 - 4x$
   (d) $y = 2 - x^2$ and $y = x$
   (e) $y = x^2 + 2$ and $x + y = 8$
   (f) $y = 9 - x^2$ and $2x + y = 6$
   (g) $y = x^2 + 4x + 1$ and $y = x - 1$
   (h) $y = x^2 - 2x + 1$ and $x + y = 3$.

4 Equations

2   Solve these simultaneous equations graphically.
    Take values of x from -4 to 4.
    (a) $y = x^2$ and $y = x + 6$
    (b) $y = x^2 + 1$ and $y = 3x - 1$
    (c) $y = x^2 - 2$ and $y = 1 - 2x$
    (d) $y = 4 - x^2$ and $y = 4x + 7$
    (e) $y = 3 - x^2$ and $x + y = 1$
    (f) $y = x^2 + 8$ and $3x + y = 6$
    (g) $y = x^2 - 2x$ and $y = 2x - 3$
    (h) $y = x^2 - 6x + 10$ and $x + y = 4$.

3   (a) Draw the graph of $y = x^2 - x - 5$. Take values of x from -4 to 4.
    (b) By drawing a suitable straight line, solve the quadratic equation $x^2 - 2x - 3 = 0$.

4   (a) Draw the graph of $y = x^2 + 3x + 1$. Take values of x from -4 to 4.
    (b) By drawing a suitable straight line, solve the quadratic equation $x^2 + x - 4 = 0$.
    Give your solutions correct to 1 decimal place.

5   (a) Find graphically the coordinates of the point of intersection of the parabola with equation $y = x^2 + 2$ and the line with equation $y = 2x + 1$. (The line is a **tangent** to the parabola.)
    (b) Use your answer to part (a) to solve the simultaneous equations $y = x^2 + 2$ and $y = 2x + 1$.

■ **You can use algebra to solve a linear equation and the equation of a parabola simultaneously.**
   - **If necessary, make y the subject of the linear equation.**
   - **Substitute for y in terms of x in the quadratic equation to obtain a quadratic equation which is entirely in terms of x.**
   - **Rearrange this quadratic equation so that you have 0 on one side.**
   - **Solve the quadratic equation.**

In this chapter, all the quadratic equations can be solved by factorization.

Example 4

(a) Solve algebraically the simultaneous equations
    $y = x^2 - 2$ and $y = 3x + 2$.
(b) Interpret your solutions geometrically.

(a) Substitute $3x + 2$ for y in the quadratic equation to obtain a quadratic equation which is entirely in terms of x: $3x + 2 = x^2 - 2$

Rearrange this quadratic equation so that it has 0 on one side: $x^2 - 3x - 4 = 0$

Factorize the left-hand side: $(x - 4)(x + 1) = 0$

State the values of x: $x = 4$ or $x = -1$

Substitute each value of x into one of the
original equations to find the corresponding
value of y:
$\quad$ when $x = 4$, $y = 3 \times 4 + 2 = 14$
$\quad$ when $x = -1$, $y = 3 \times -1 + 2 = -1$

> Check that this pair of solutions also satisfy $y = x^2 - 2$.

The solutions are $x = 4$, $y = 14$ and $x = -1$, $y = -1$.

(b) The coordinates of the points of intersection of the line with equation $y = 3x + 2$ and the parabola with equation $y = x^2 - 2$ are $(4, 14)$ and $(-1, -1)$.

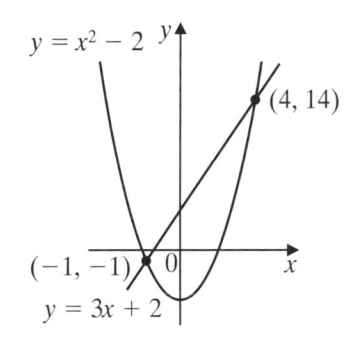

Example 5

(a) Solve algebraically the simultaneous equations $y = x^2 + 4$ and $y = 2x + 3$.
(b) Interpret your solutions geometrically.

(a) Substitute $2x + 3$ for y in the quadratic equation to obtain a quadratic equation which is entirely in terms of x: $\quad 2x + 3 = x^2 + 4$

Rearrange this quadratic equation so that it has 0 on one side: $\quad x^2 - 2x + 1 = 0$

Factorize the left-hand side: $\quad (x - 1)^2 = 0$

State the value of x: $\quad x = 1$

Substitute $x = 1$ into one of the original equations to find the corresponding value of y: $\quad$ when $x = 1$, $y = 2 \times 1 + 3 = 5$
The solution is $x = 1$, $y = 5$.

> Check that this solution also satisfies $y = x^2 + 4$.

(b) The parabola with equation $y = x^2 + 4$ and the line with equation $y = 2x + 3$ meet only at the point with coordinates $(1, 5)$. The line touches the parabola and is a **tangent** to the parabola.

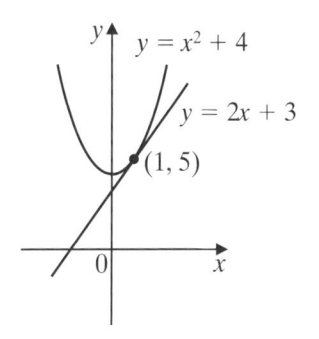

6 Equations

Example 6

Solve algebraically the simultaneous equations
$y = 3x^2 + 8$ and $5x + y = 10$.

Make y the subject of the linear equation: $\quad y = 10 - 5x$

Substitute $10 - 5x$ for y in the quadratic
equation to obtain a quadratic equation
which is entirely in terms of x: $\quad 10 - 5x = 3x^2 + 8$

Rearrange this quadratic equation so
that it has 0 on one side: $\quad 3x^2 + 5x - 2 = 0$

Factorize the left-hand side: $\quad (x + 2)(3x - 1) = 0$

State the values of x: $\quad x = -2$ or $x = \frac{1}{3}$

Substitute each value of x
into one of the original
equations to find the
corresponding value of y: when $x = -2$, $y = 10 - 5 \times -2 = 20$
when $x = \frac{1}{3}$, $y = 10 - 5 \times \frac{1}{3} = 8\frac{1}{3}$

The solutions are $x = -2, y = 20$ and $x = \frac{1}{3}, y = 8\frac{1}{3}$.

> Check that this pair of solutions also satisfy $y = 3x^2 + 8$.

Exercise 1B Links 21G

1 Solve the simultaneous equations:
(a) $y = x^2$ and $y = 5x - 4$
(b) $y = x^2$ and $y = 4x + 5$
(c) $y = x^2 + 1$ and $y = 9 - 2x$
(d) $y = x^2 - 8$ and $x + y = 12$
(e) $y = 9 - x^2$ and $y = 3x - 1$
(f) $y = x^2 - 3$ and $3x + y = 15$
(g) $y = x^2 + 9x + 4$ and $y = x - 3$
(h) $y = x^2 + 2x - 4$ and $y = 10 - 3x$.

2 Solve the simultaneous equations:
(a) $y = 2x^2$ and $y = 7x - 3$
(b) $y = 3x^2$ and $x + y = 2$
(c) $y = 5x^2 + 2$ and $y = 2x + 5$
(d) $y = 2x^2 - 7$ and $y = x + 3$
(e) $y = 6 - 4x^2$ and $y = 4x + 3$
(f) $y = 12x^2 + 7$ and $5x + y = 10$
(g) $y = 6x^2 - 3x - 1$ and $y = 2x + 3$
(h) $y = 10x^2 + x - 13$ and $y = 5 - 2x$.

3 Find the coordinates of the points of intersection of these lines and parabolas:
(a) $y = x^2 + 6$ and $y = 7x - 4$
(b) $y = 4 - x^2$ and $y = 8x - 5$
(c) $y = 2x^2$ and $y = 3x + 5$
(d) $y = 5x^2 + 2$ and $y = 18x - 7$
(e) $y = 3x^2 - 7x + 3$ and $y = 6x - 1$
(f) $y = 6x^2 + 6x + 5$ and $x + y = 3$
(g) $y = 12x^2 + x + 5$ and $10x + y = 20$.

4 The line with equation $y = 6x - 1$ is a tangent to the parabola with equation $y = x^2 + 8$.
Find the coordinates of the point at which the line touches the parabola.

5 (a) Solve algebraically the simultaneous equations
$4x + 2y = 19$ and $y = 9 - 2x^2$.
(b) Interpret your solutions geometrically.

1.2 The intersection of a line and a circle

- $x^2 + y^2 = r^2$ is the equation of a circle, centre the origin and radius r. For example, $x^2 + y^2 = 16$ is the equation of a circle centre the origin and radius 4 units.
- You can find the coordinates of the points of intersection of a line and a circle graphically.
- You can solve a linear equation and an equation of a circle simultaneously by drawing the line and the circle.
  Their points of intersection represent the common solutions.

Example 7
(a) Find graphically the points of intersection of the line with equation $y = 2x - 5$ and the circle with equation $x^2 + y^2 = 25$.
(b) Use your answer to part (a) to solve the simultaneous equations $y = 2x - 5$ and $x^2 + y^2 = 25$.

If you don't use the same scale on each axis, you won't get a circle!

(a) Plot three points for $y = 2x - 5$,
e.g. (3, 1), (4, 3) and (5, 5).
$x^2 + y^2 = 25$ is the equation of a circle centre the origin with a radius of 5 units.
The coordinates of the points of intersection are (4, 3) and (0, −5).
(b) The points of intersection represent the solutions of the simultaneous equations $y = 2x - 5$ and $x^2 + y^2 = 25$.
So the solutions are
$x = 4, y = 3$ and $x = 0, y = -5$.

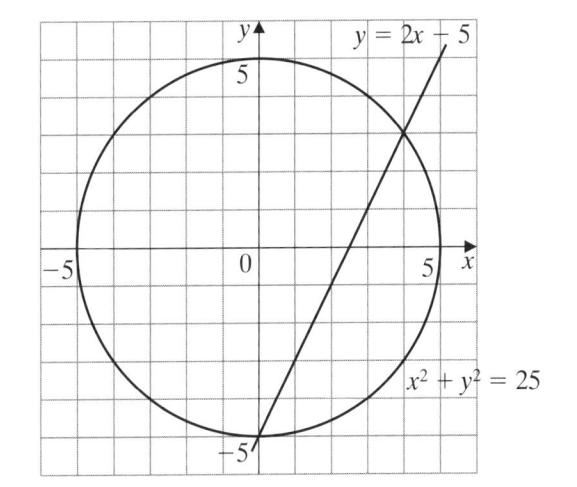

8 Equations

Example 8

Solve graphically the simultaneous equations $x+y = 2$ and $x^2 + y^2 = 100$.

Plot three points for $x+y = 2$, e.g. (0, 2), (1, 1) and (2, 0).
$x^2 + y^2 = 100$ is the equation of a circle centre the origin with a radius of 10 units.

The points of intersection represent the solutions of the simultaneous equations $x+y = 2$ and $x^2 + y^2 = 100$.
So the solutions are
$x = 8, y = -6$
and
$x = -6, y = 8$.

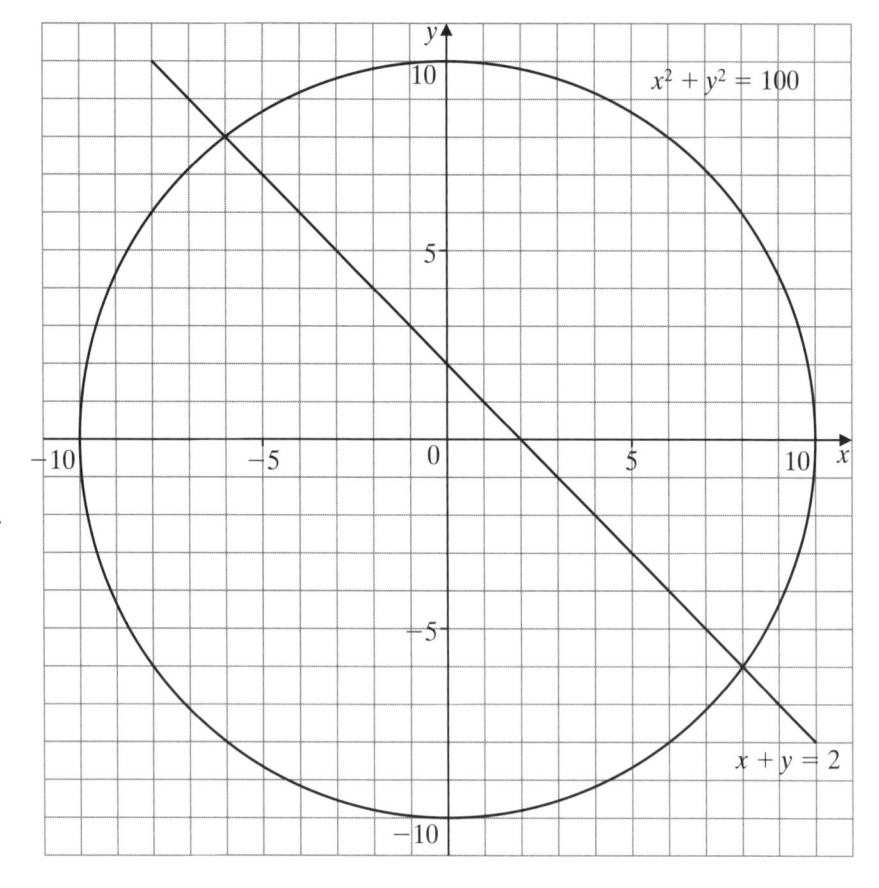

Exercise 1C

1. Find graphically the coordinates of the points of intersection of these circles and lines:
   (a) $y = x + 1$ and $x^2 + y^2 = 25$
   (b) $y = 3x - 10$ and $x^2 + y^2 = 100$
   (c) $x + y = 1$ and $x^2 + y^2 = 25$
   (d) $x + 2y = 20$ and $x^2 + y^2 = 100$
   (e) $y = 3 - x$ and $x^2 + y^2 = 9$.

2. Solve these simultaneous equations graphically:
   (a) $y = x - 2$ and $x^2 + y^2 = 100$
   (b) $y = 3x + 5$ and $x^2 + y^2 = 25$
   (c) $x + y + 1 = 0$ and $x^2 + y^2 = 25$
   (d) $2y - x = 20$ and $x^2 + y^2 = 100$
   (e) $x + y = 4$ and $x^2 + y^2 = 16$.

3. (a) Find graphically the coordinates of the point of intersection of the line with equation $3x - 4y = 50$ and the circle with equation $x^2 + y^2 = 100$. (The line is a tangent to the circle.)
   (b) Use your answer to part (a) to solve the simultaneous equations $3x - 4y = 50$ and $x^2 + y^2 = 100$.

- You can use algebra to solve a linear equation and an equation of a circle simultaneously.
  - If necessary, make y or x (whichever is simpler) the subject of the linear equation.
  - Substitute for y in terms of x (or x in terms of y) in the quadratic equation to obtain a quadratic equation which is entirely in terms of one letter.
  - Expand the brackets.
  - Simplify the quadratic equation and rearrange it so that you have 0 on one side.
  - If there is a common factor, divide every term by it.
  - Solve the quadratic equation.

In this chapter, all the quadratic equations can be solved by factorization.

Example 9

(a) Solve algebraically the simultaneous equations $y = x + 3$ and $x^2 + y^2 = 17$.

(b) Interpret your solutions geometrically.

(a) Substitute $x + 3$ for y in the quadratic equation to obtain a quadratic equation which is entirely in terms of x: $\quad x^2 + (x+3)^2 = 17$

Expand the brackets: $\quad x^2 + x^2 + 6x + 9 = 17$

Simplify the quadratic equation and rearrange it so that it has 0 on one side: $\quad 2x^2 + 6x - 8 = 0$

2 is a common factor. So divide every term by 2: $\quad x^2 + 3x - 4 = 0$

Factorize the left-hand side: $\quad (x-1)(x+4) = 0$

State the values of x: $\quad x = 1 \text{ or } x = -4$

Substitute each value of x into one of the original equations to find the corresponding value of y: when $x = 1$, $y = 1 + 3 = 4$
when $x = -4$, $y = -4 + 3 = -1$

The solutions are $x = 1, y = 4$ and $x = -4, y = -1$.

Check that this pair of solutions also satisfy $x^2 + y^2 = 17$.

(b) The coordinates of the points of intersection of the line with equation $y = x + 3$ and the circle with equation $x^2 + y^2 = 17$ are $(1, 4)$ and $(-4, -1)$.

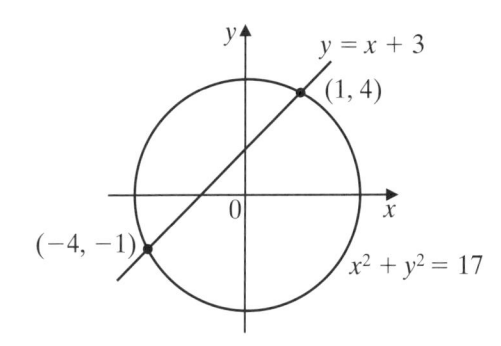

10 Equations

Example 10

(a) Solve algebraically the simultaneous equations $2x + y = 10$ and $x^2 + y^2 = 20$.

(b) Interpret your solutions geometrically.

(a) Make y the subject of the linear equation:
$$y = 10 - 2x$$

Substitute $10 - 2x$ for y in the quadratic equation to obtain a quadratic equation which is entirely in terms of x:
$$x^2 + (10 - 2x)^2 = 20$$

Expand the brackets:
$$x^2 + 100 - 40x + 4x^2 = 20$$

Simplify the quadratic equation and rearrange it so that it has 0 on one side:
$$5x^2 - 40x + 80 = 0$$

5 is a common factor. So divide every term by 5:
$$x^2 - 8x + 16 = 0$$

Factorize the left-hand side:
$$(x - 4)^2 = 0$$

State the value of x:
$$x = 4$$

Substitute $x = 4$ into one of the original equations to find the corresponding value of y:

when $x = 4$, $2 \times 4 + y = 10$
so $y = 2$
The solution is $x = 4$, $y = 2$.

> Check that this solution also satisfies $x^2 + y^2 = 20$.

(b) The line with equation $2x + y = 10$ and the circle with equation $x^2 + y^2 = 20$ meet only at the point with coordinates $(4, 2)$. So the line is a tangent to the circle.

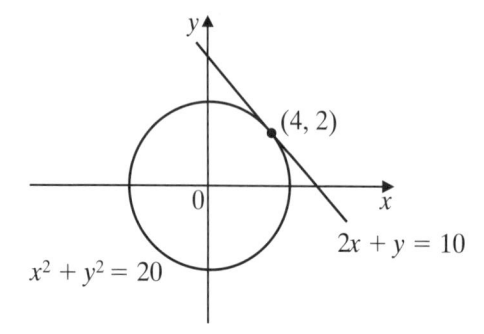

Example 11

Solve algebraically the simultaneous equations $x - 2y = 3$ and $x^2 + y^2 = 41$.

Make x the subject of the linear equation:
$$x = 2y + 3$$

Substitute $2y + 3$ for x in the quadratic equation to obtain a quadratic equation which is entirely in terms of y:
$$(2y + 3)^2 + y^2 = 41$$

> You could substitute $\frac{x-3}{2}$ for y but this would make the algebra more awkward.

Expand the brackets: $\qquad 4y^2 + 12y + 9 + y^2 = 41$

Simplify the quadratic equation and
rearrange it so that it has 0 on one side: $\qquad 5y^2 + 12y - 32 = 0$

Factorize the left-hand side: $\qquad (5y - 8)(y + 4) = 0$

State the values of y: $\qquad y = 1\frac{3}{5}$ or $y = -4$

Substitute each value of y into one of the original equations to find
the corresponding value of x: when $y = 1\frac{3}{5}$, $x = 2 \times 1\frac{3}{5} + 3 = 6\frac{1}{5}$

when $y = -4$, $x = 2 \times -4 + 3 = -5$

The solutions are $x = 6\frac{1}{5}$, $y = 1\frac{3}{5}$ and $x = -5$, $y = -4$.

> Check that this pair of solutions also satisfy $x^2 + y^2 = 41$.

Exercise 1D   Links 21H

1 Solve the simultaneous equations:
   (a) $y = x + 1$ and $x^2 + y^2 = 13$
   (b) $y = x - 2$ and $x^2 + y^2 = 34$
   (c) $x + y = 3$ and $x^2 + y^2 = 45$
   (d) $x - y = 7$ and $x^2 + y^2 = 49$
   (e) $y = 2x - 3$ and $x^2 + y^2 = 5$
   (f) $x - 2y = 1$ and $x^2 + y^2 = 2$.

2 Solve the simultaneous equations and interpret your solutions geometrically:
   (a) $y = 2$ and $x^2 + y^2 = 40$
   (b) $y = x + 6$ and $x^2 + y^2 = 50$
   (c) $y = x - 5$ and $x^2 + y^2 = 17$
   (d) $y = x + 4$ and $x^2 + y^2 = 8$
   (e) $y = 3x + 1$ and $x^2 + y^2 = 29$
   (f) $x + y = 6$ and $x^2 + y^2 = 18$
   (g) $3x + y = 2$ and $x^2 + y^2 = 20$
   (h) $x - 2y = 1$ and $x^2 + y^2 = 65$.

3 The line with equation $3y + 2x = 13$ is a tangent to the circle with equation $x^2 + y^2 = 13$. Find the coordinates of the point at which the line touches the circle.

Exercise 1E   Mixed questions

1 Solve these simultaneous equations graphically.
   Take values of x from -5 to 5.
   (a) $y = x^2 - 8$ and $y = x + 4$
   (b) $y = x^2 + 2$ and $y = 7 - 4x$
   (c) $y = 3 - x^2$ and $y = 2x - 5$
   (d) $y = x^2 + 3x + 5$ and $x + y = 2$.

2 Solve these simultaneous equations graphically:
(a) $y = x - 1$ and $x^2 + y^2 = 25$
(b) $y = x + 2$ and $x^2 + y^2 = 100$
(c) $x + 3y = 15$ and $x^2 + y^2 = 25$
(d) $x + y + 2 = 0$ and $x^2 + y^2 = 100$.

3 Solve these simultaneous equations algebraically:
(a) $y = x^2 - 6$ and $y = 3x + 4$
(b) $y = x^2 + 3x - 5$ and $y = 1 - 2x$
(c) $y = 2x^2 - 7$ and $y = 2x + 5$
(d) $y = x^2 + 2$ and $y = 7 - 4x$
(e) $y = 2x + 5$ and $x^2 + y^2 = 10$
(f) $x + y = 4$ and $x^2 + y^2 = 58$
(g) $3y - x = 2$ and $x^2 + y^2 = 20$
(h) $x - y = 5$ and $x^2 + y^2 = 73$.

4 Solve these simultaneous equations algebraically and interpret the solutions geometrically:
(a) $y = 3x^2 - 1$ and $y = x + 1$
(b) $y = 1 - x^2$ and $4x + y = 5$
(c) $3x + y = 20$ and $x^2 + y^2 = 40$
(d) $y = 2x - 7$ and $x^2 + y^2 = 17$.

5 (a) Draw the graph of $y = x^2 - 4x + 1$.
Take values of x from -3 to 7.
(b) By drawing a suitable straight line, solve the quadratic equation $x^2 - 4x - 7 = 0$. Give your solutions correct to 1 decimal place.
(c) By drawing a suitable straight line, solve the quadratic equation $x^2 - 6x + 6 = 0$. Give your solutions correct to 1 decimal place.

6 (a) The line with equation $x + y = 8$ is a tangent to the circle with equation $x^2 + y^2 = 32$. Find algebraically the coordinates of the point at which the line touches the circle.
(b) The line with equation $x + y = c$ is a tangent to the circle with equation $x^2 + y^2 = r^2$. Show that $c^2 = 2r^2$.

Summary of key points

- You can find the coordinates of the points of intersection of a line and a parabola graphically.
- You can solve a linear equation and a quadratic equation simultaneously by drawing the graphs for the equations. Their points of intersection represent the common solutions.

- You can solve a quadratic equation by finding the x-coordinates of the points of intersection of a parabola and a straight line.
- You can use algebra to solve a linear equation and the equation of a parabola simultaneously.
  - If necessary, make y the subject of the linear equation.
  - Substitute for y in terms of x in the quadratic equation to obtain a quadratic equation which is entirely in terms of x.
  - Rearrange this quadratic equation so that you have 0 on one side.
  - Solve the quadratic equation.
- $x^2 + y^2 = r^2$ is the equation of a circle, centre the origin and radius r. For example, $x^2 + y^2 = 16$ is the equation of a circle centre the origin and radius 4 units.
- You can find the coordinates of the points of intersection of a line and a circle graphically.
- You can solve a linear equation and an equation of a circle simultaneously by drawing the line and the circle. Their points of intersection represent the common solutions.
- You can use algebra to solve a linear equation and an equation of a circle simultaneously.
  - If necessary, make y or x (whichever is simpler) the subject of the linear equation.
  - Substitute for y in terms of x (or x in terms of y) in the quadratic equation to obtain a quadratic equation which is entirely in terms of one letter.
  - Expand the brackets.
  - Simplify the quadratic equation and rearrange it so that you have 0 on one side.
  - If there is a common factor, divide every term by it.
  - Solve the quadratic equation.

2 Powers, proportion and calculator methods

2.1 Powers and indices

- In the expression x^n the number x is called the *base* and the number n is called the *index* or *power*.
- $x^m \times x^n = x^{m+n}$
- $(x^m)^n = x^{mn}$
- $x^m \div x^n = x^{m-n}$
- $x^1 = x$
- $x^0 = 1$ when $x \neq 0$
- $x^{-n} = \dfrac{1}{x^n}$
- $x^{\frac{1}{2}} = \sqrt{x}$
- $x^{\frac{1}{n}} = \sqrt[n]{x}$
- $x^{\frac{m}{n}} = \left(\sqrt[n]{x}\right)^m$ or $\sqrt[n]{x^m}$

Example 1
(a) Simplify $x^2 \times x^5$.
(b) Simplify $n^8 \div n^3$.
(c) Simplify $\dfrac{12p^6}{3p \times 2p^3}$.

(a) We simply add the indices, so $x^2 \times x^5 = x^{2+5} = x^7$
(b) We simply subtract the indices, so $n^8 \div n^3 = n^{8-3} = n^5$
(c) We have $\dfrac{12p^6}{3p \times 2p^3} = \dfrac{12p^6}{6p^4} = 2p^2$

Example 2
Without evaluating them, list these numbers in order, starting with the smallest:

$$2^{10} \quad 8^3 \quad 4^7 \quad 16^4 \quad \sqrt{2^{24}}$$

Write each with a base of 2:

$8^3 = (2^3)^3 = 2^9$

$4^7 = (2^2)^7 = 2^{14}$

$16^4 = (2^4)^4 = 2^{16}$

$\sqrt{2^{24}} = (2^{24})^{\frac{1}{2}} = 2^{12}$

So the correct order is 2^9 2^{10} 2^{12} 2^{14} 2^{16}

i.e. 8^3 2^{10} $\sqrt{2^{24}}$ 4^7 16^4

Example 3
(a) Work out $8^{\frac{2}{3}}$
(b) Work out $32^{\frac{1}{5}}$

(a) $8^{\frac{2}{3}} = \sqrt[3]{8^2} = 4$
(b) $32^{\frac{1}{5}} = \sqrt[5]{32} = 2$

Exercise 2A

1 Simplify:
   (a) $x^4 \times x^2$
   (b) $3x^7 \div x^2$
   (c) $\dfrac{24x^5}{3x^2 \times 2x}$

2 Work out $\left(\dfrac{125}{27}\right)^{-\frac{1}{3}}$.

3 Without evaluating them, list these numbers in order, starting with the smallest:
   $\sqrt[3]{3^{15}}$ 3^{-10} 9^4 27^2

4 Work out:
   (a) $25^{\frac{1}{2}}$
   (b) $(36)^{\frac{3}{2}}$
   (c) $16^{-\frac{3}{4}}$

5 (a) Simplify $x^3 \times x^5$
   (b) Simplify $y^6 \div y^2$
   (c) Simplify $\dfrac{8w^7}{2w^2 \times w^3}$

6 (a) Simplify $(3xy^3)^4$
   (b) Find the value of $\left(\dfrac{64}{125}\right)^{-\frac{1}{3}}$
   (c) Work out $8^{-\frac{1}{3}} \times (36)^{\frac{1}{2}}$

7 (a) Solve the equation
   $$3^{2x-1} = \tfrac{1}{27}$$
   (b) Simplify $\dfrac{(5x^2y)^3}{15xy}$

8 Evaluate:
   (a) 5^{-2}
   (b) $8^{\frac{2}{3}}$
   (c) $49^{-\frac{1}{2}}$

2.2 Surds

- A number written exactly using square roots is called a *surd*. For example $\sqrt{3}$ and $2 - \sqrt{5}$ are in surd form.
- $\sqrt{a \times b} = \sqrt{a} \times \sqrt{b}$
- $\sqrt{\dfrac{a}{b}} = \dfrac{\sqrt{a}}{\sqrt{b}}$
- A simplified (or 'rationalized') surd should never have a square root in its denominator.

Example 4
Solve the equation
$$x^2 - 2 = 25$$
leaving your answer in the most simplified surd form.

$$x^2 - 2 = 25$$
so $\quad x^2 = 25 + 2 = 27$
$\quad x = \pm\sqrt{27} = \pm\sqrt{9 \times 3}$
so $\quad x = \pm 3\sqrt{3}$

> Try not to forget the $\pm$.

Example 5
Solve the equation
$$x^2 - 6x - 11 = 0$$

Leave your answer in the most simplified surd form.

Completing the square on $x^2 - 6x - 11 = 0$ gives
$$(x-3)^2 - 9 - 11 = 0$$
so
$$(x-3)^2 = 20$$
$$(x-3) = \pm\sqrt{20}$$
$$x - 3 = \pm\sqrt{4 \times 5} = \pm 2\sqrt{5}$$
$$x = 3 + 2\sqrt{5} \quad \text{or} \quad x = 3 - 2\sqrt{5}$$

Example 6
Simplify: (a) $\dfrac{1}{\sqrt{7}}$ (b) $\dfrac{50}{\sqrt{5}}$

(a) Multiplying $\dfrac{1}{\sqrt{7}}$ by $\dfrac{\sqrt{7}}{\sqrt{7}}$ gives $\dfrac{1}{\sqrt{7}} \times \dfrac{\sqrt{7}}{\sqrt{7}} = \dfrac{\sqrt{7}}{7}$

(b) $\dfrac{50}{\sqrt{5}} = \dfrac{5 \times 10}{\sqrt{5}} = \sqrt{5} \times 10 = 10\sqrt{5}$

Example 7
Simplify $(3 - \sqrt{5})^2$, giving your answer in the form $a + n\sqrt{b}$.

$$(3 - \sqrt{5})^2 = (3 - \sqrt{5})(3 - \sqrt{5}) = 3 \times 3 - 3 \times \sqrt{5} - 3 \times \sqrt{5} + \sqrt{5} \times \sqrt{5}$$
$$= 9 - 2 \times 3\sqrt{5} + 5$$
$$= 9 + 5 - 6\sqrt{5}$$
$$= 14 - 6\sqrt{5}$$

Exercise 2B

1. Solve the equation
$$x^2 + 8x - 12 = 0$$
Leave your answer in surd form.

2. Rationalize:
    (a) $\dfrac{1}{\sqrt{5}}$
    (b) $\dfrac{2}{\sqrt{3}}$
    (c) $\dfrac{14}{\sqrt{7}}$
    (d) $\dfrac{20}{\sqrt{5}}$

3. Simplify:
    (a) $(4 + \sqrt{3})^2$
    (b) $(5 - \sqrt{2})(5 + \sqrt{2})$
    (c) $(7 - \sqrt{5})^2$

4. (a) Find the value of:
    (i) m when $\sqrt{128} = 2^m$
    (ii) n when $(\sqrt{8} - \sqrt{2})^2 = 2^n$.
   (b) A rectangle has a length of 2^t cm and a width of $(\sqrt{8} - \sqrt{2})$ cm. The area of the rectangle is $\sqrt{128}$ cm². Find t.

5. Simplify $\dfrac{(7 - 3\sqrt{2})^2}{(3 - \sqrt{2})(3 + \sqrt{2})}$.

6. Solve the equation
$$x^2 - 2 = 70$$
leaving your answer in surd form.

7. Expand $(1 + \sqrt{3})^2$, giving your answer in the form $a + n\sqrt{b}$.

8. The solution to a simple quadratic equation is
$$x = \pm 2\sqrt{5}$$
Write down the quadratic equation in its simplest form.

2.3 Proportion

- The symbol $\propto$ means 'is proportional to'.
- $y \propto x$ means y is directly proportional to x.
- When a graph connecting two quantities is a straight line through the origin then one quantity is directly proportional to the other.
- When y is directly proportional to x, a proportionality statement and a formula connecting y and x can be written:
  - $y \propto x$ is the proportionality statement
  - $y = kx$ is the proportionality formula, where k is a constant of proportionality.
- When y is directly proportional to the square of x:
  - $y \propto x^2$ is the proportionality statement
  - $y = kx^2$ is the proportionality formula, where k is the constant of proportionality.
- When y is directly proportional to the cube of x:
  - $y \propto x^3$ is the proportionality statement
  - $y = kx^3$ is the proportionality formula, where k is the constant of proportionality.
- When y is inversely proportional to x:
  - $y \propto \dfrac{1}{x}$ is the proportionality statement
  - $y = k \times \dfrac{1}{x}$ or $y = \dfrac{k}{x}$ are ways of writing the proportionality formula, where k is the constant of inverse proportionality.
- When y is inversely proportional to x^2:

$$y = \frac{k}{x^2} \quad \left(\text{i.e. } y \propto \frac{1}{x^2}\right)$$

Example 8

y is inversely proportional to x^2.
$y = 8$ when $x = 3$.

(a) Write y in terms of x.
(b) Calculate the value of y when $x = 2$.
(c) Calculate the exact values of x when $y = 7.2$.

(a) $y \propto \dfrac{1}{x^2}$ so $y = \dfrac{k}{x^2}$

When $x = 3, y = 8$.

So $8 = \dfrac{k}{9}$ $k = 8 \times 9 = 72$

so $y = \dfrac{72}{x^2}$

(b) $y = \dfrac{72}{x^2} = \dfrac{72}{4}$

so $y = 18$.

(c) $7.2 = \dfrac{72}{x^2}$

so $x^2 = \dfrac{72}{7.2} \quad x^2 = 10$

$x = \pm\sqrt{10}$

Try to remember the $\pm$.

Example 9

Match each of these statements:

    1 y is directly proportional to x

    2 y is directly proportional to x^2

    3 y is inversely proportional to x

to one of these sketch graphs:

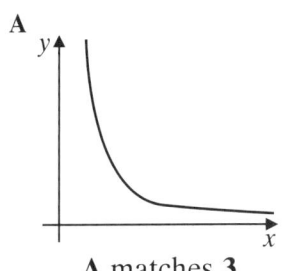

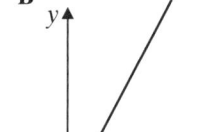

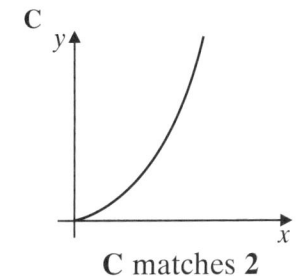

A   **B**   **C**

   A matches **3**   **B** matches **1**   **C** matches **2**

Exercise 2C

1 y is directly proportional to $\sqrt{x}$.
When $x = 9$, $y = 15$.
Write y in terms of x.

2 y is inversely proportional to x.
When $y = 3$, $x = 10$.
Find y in terms of x.

3 y is inversely proportional to x^2.
$y = 3$ when $x = 4$.
    (a) Write y in terms of x.
    (b) Calculate the value of y when $x = 5$.
    (c) Calculate the value of x when $y = 12$.

4 y is directly proportional to x^2.
$y = 12$ when $x = 6$.
    (a) Calculate y when $x = 5$.
    (b) Calculate x when $y = 8$.

20 Powers, proportion and calculator methods

5 y is inversely proportional to x.
Sketch the graph of y against x.

6 y is directly proportional to x^3. $y = 40$ when $x = 2$.
   (a) Express y in terms of x.
   (b) Calculate y when $x = 3$.

7 y is inversely proportional to x^2.
$y = 2$ when $x = \sqrt{3}$.
Work out the value of y when $x = 2$.

8 y is inversely proportional to x.
$y = 3$ when $x = 2$.
Prove that $xy = 6$.

9 y is directly proportional to $x^{\frac{1}{2}}$. When $x = 16$, $y = 20$.
Work out the value of y when $x = 25$.

10 s is inversely proportional to t^2.
$s = 12$ when $t = 1$.
   (a) Work out s when $t = 2$.
   (b) Work out t when $s = 4$.

11 The cost of a square rug is directly proportional to the length of a side of the rug.
When the length of a side of the square rug is 4 m, the cost of the rug is £160.
Work out the cost of a similar square rug of side length 3 m.

12 The mass of a cube is directly proportional to the length of a side of the cube. The mass of the cube is 32 grams when the length of a side is 2 centimetres.
   (a) Calculate the mass of a similar cube when the length of a side is 5 cm.
   (b) Calculate the length of a side of a similar cube when the mass is 4 kg.

2.4 Efficient and effective use of a calculator

- **Calculators should be used efficiently and effectively.**
- **A number can be efficiently raised to any power by the x^y button.**
- **The nth root of any number can be efficiently found by using the $\sqrt{}$ button.**

Your teacher can help you if your calculator uses different buttons.

Example 10
Use your calculator to work out the value of

$$\frac{\sqrt{15.7^3 - 800.1}}{12.8 \times 3.78}$$

Give your answer correct to 2 decimal places.

$15.7^3 - 800.1 = 3869.893 - 800.1 = 3069.793$

$\sqrt{3069.793} = 55.4057127$

$55.4057127 \div 12.8 = 4.328571305$

$4.328571305 \div 3.78 = 1.145124684$

which correct to 2 decimal places is 1.15.

> 15.7^3 can be found using the x^3 function.

Example 11

Louise bought a car valued at £12 000.
The value of the car depreciates at a rate of 15% per year.

Work out the value of the car 6 years after Louise bought it.

To depreciate by 15% per year means that at the end of a year the value of the car is 0.85 of its value at the start of the year.

So after 6 years the value of the car is $(0.85)^6 \times 12\,000$.

Value after 6 years is £4525.79 (to nearest penny).

> Find $(0.85)^6$ using the x^y function, with $x = 0.85$ and $y = 6$.

Exercise 2D

1. Use your calculator to work out:

   $$\frac{27.6 - 3.8^2}{5.2 - \sqrt{2.56}}$$

2. Use your calculator to work out the value of

   $$\frac{\sqrt{12.3^2 + 7.9}}{1.8 \times 0.17}$$

   Give your answer correct to 1 decimal place.

3. The price of a new television is £423.
   This price includes Value Added Tax (VAT) at $17\frac{1}{2}\%$.
   (a) Work out the cost of the television **before** VAT was added.

   By the end of each year, the value of a television has fallen by 12% of its value at the start of that year.
   The value of a television was £423 at the start of the first year.
   (b) Work out the value of the television at the end of the **third** year.
   Give your answer to the nearest penny.

4. James and Donna bought a new flat for £130 000.
   The value of the flat appreciated by 8% per year.
   Work out the value of the flat 7 years after it was bought by James and Donna.

22 Powers, proportion and calculator methods

5 Use your calculator to work out the value of
$$\frac{(17.42^2 + 8.3)^{\frac{1}{3}}}{\sqrt{1.86 \times 3.54}}$$
Give your answer correct to 1 place of decimals.

6 Use your calculator to work out the value of
$$(17.38)^{\frac{1}{5}}$$

7 Sumreen bought a new motorcycle for £8000 on 1 July 1998. The value of the motorcycle depreciates by 12% per year. Work out the value of the motorcycle on 1 July 2006.

Exercise 2E   Mixed questions

1 Simplify:
  (a) $x^7 \times x^2$
  (b) $x^6 \div x^4$
  (c) $(3n)^2$
  (d) $(4p^2q)^2$
  (e) $\dfrac{12m^5}{3m \times 4m^2}$
  (f) $\dfrac{y^3}{y^7}$

2 Work out:
  (a) $(25)^{\frac{1}{2}}$
  (b) $1000^{-\frac{1}{3}}$
  (c) $8^{-\frac{2}{3}}$

3 Solve the equation $3^{2x-1} = 243$.

4 Evaluate:
  (a) 7^0
  (b) $(36)^{-\frac{1}{2}}$
  (c) $\left(\dfrac{9}{16}\right)^{\frac{1}{2}}$

5 Write these in order, starting with the smallest:
  $3^5 \qquad 9^4 \qquad 27^2 \qquad (9^{\frac{1}{2}})^4$

6 Simplify:
  (a) $\dfrac{1}{\sqrt{13}}$
  (b) $\dfrac{42}{\sqrt{6}}$

7 Expand $(2 + \sqrt{5})^2$, giving your answer in the form $a + n\sqrt{b}$.

8 Solve the equation $x^2 - 6x - 15 = 0$, giving your answer in surd form.

9 y is directly proportional to x^3.
  When $x = 2$, $y = 40$.
  (a) Work out y when $x = 3$.
  (b) Work out x when $y = \frac{5}{8}$.

10 Use your calculator to work out $\dfrac{\sqrt{4.83^3 - 1.62^4}}{12.8 \times 23.4}$.

Summary of key points

- In the expression x^n the number x is called the *base* and the number n is called the *index* or *power*.
- $x^m \times x^n = x^{m+n}$
- $(x^m)^n = x^{mn}$
- $x^m \div x^n = x^{m-n}$
- $x^1 = x$
- $x^0 = 1$ when $x \neq 0$
- $x^{-n} = \dfrac{1}{x^n}$
- $x^{\frac{1}{2}} = \sqrt{x}$
- $x^{\frac{1}{n}} = \sqrt[n]{x}$
- $x^{\frac{m}{n}} = \left(\sqrt[n]{x}\right)^m$ or $\sqrt[n]{x^m}$
- A number written exactly using square roots is called a *surd*. For example $\sqrt{3}$ and $2 - \sqrt{5}$ are in surd form.
- $\sqrt{a \times b} = \sqrt{a} \times \sqrt{b}$
- $\sqrt{\dfrac{a}{b}} = \dfrac{\sqrt{a}}{\sqrt{b}}$
- A simplified (or 'rationalized') surd should never have a square root in its denominator.
- The symbol $\propto$ means 'is proportional to'.
- $y \propto x$ means y is directly proportional to x.
- When a graph connecting two quantities is a straight line through the origin then one quantity is directly proportional to the other.
- When y is directly proportional to x, a proportionality statement and a formula connecting y and x can be written:
  - $y \propto x$ is the proportionality statement
  - $y = kx$ is the proportionality formula, where k is a constant of proportionality.
- When y is directly proportional to the square of x:
  - $y \propto x^2$ is the proportionality statement
  - $y = kx^2$ is the proportionality formula, where k is the constant of proportionality.
- When y is directly proportional to the cube of x:
  - $y \propto x^3$ is the proportionality statement
  - $y = kx^3$ is the proportionality formula, where k is the constant of proportionality.

- When y is inversely proportional to x:
  - $y \propto \dfrac{1}{x}$ is the proportionality statement
  - $y = k \times \dfrac{1}{x}$ or $y = \dfrac{k}{x}$ are ways of writing the proportionality formula, where k is the constant of inverse proportionality.
- When y is inversely proportional to x^2:
  $$y = \dfrac{k}{x^2} \quad \left(\text{i.e. } y \propto \dfrac{1}{x^2}\right)$$
- Calculators should be used efficiently and effectively.
- A number can be efficiently raised to any power by the x^y button.
- The nth root of any number can be efficiently found by using the $\sqrt[y]{\ }$ button.

3 Straight line and transformed graphs

3.1 Straight line graphs

- An intercept is a point at which a line cuts the y-axis or the x-axis.
- The general form of the equation of a straight line is
  $$y = mx + c$$
  where m is the gradient and $(0, c)$ is the intercept on the y-axis.
- Lines of the same gradient (m) are parallel.
- If a line has a gradient of m, a line perpendicular to it has a gradient of $\dfrac{-1}{m}$.
- If two lines are perpendicular, the product of their gradients is -1.

Example 1
The equation of a straight line is
$$4y - 3x = 12$$

(a) Find
   (i) the gradient of this line,
   (ii) the coordinates of the intercept of the line on the y-axis.

A second line is parallel to $4y - 3x = 12$ and cuts the y-axis at the point $(0, -5)$.

(b) Find the equation of this second line.

A third line is perpendicular to $4y - 3x = 12$ and passes through the point $(6, -1)$.

(c) Find the equation of this third line.

(a) Rearranging $4y - 3x = 12$ gives
$$4y = 3x + 12$$
$$y = \frac{3x}{4} + 3$$

So the gradient is $\frac{3}{4}$.
The intercept with the y-axis is at the point $(0, 3)$.

(b) The second line is parallel to the first line, so it has a gradient of $\frac{3}{4}$. Since it passes through $(0, -5)$ it has equation
$$y = \frac{3x}{4} - 5$$

(c) The third straight line is perpendicular to the first one, so the third straight line has a gradient of

$$-\frac{1}{\frac{3}{4}} = -\frac{4}{3}$$

So the equation of the third line is $y = -\frac{4x}{3} + c$.

$(6, -1)$ lies on this line, so we can substitute these values into the equation to find c:

$$-1 = -\frac{4 \times 6}{3} + c$$

$$-1 = -8 + c$$

$$c = 7$$

So the equation of the third line is

$$y = -\frac{4x}{3} + 7 \quad \text{(or } 3y + 4x = 21\text{)}$$

Exercise 3A

1 Find the gradient of a line perpendicular to
$$3x + y = 5$$

2 A line, L, is perpendicular to $2x - y = 1$ and passes through the point $(0, 5)$.
Find the equation of the line L.

3 The equations of five lines are:
(a) $y = 3x + 2$ (b) $y - x = 1$ (c) $2y - x = 3$
(d) $3x + 2y = 1$ (e) $5y - 2x = 7$
For each line, write down the gradient that is:
(i) parallel
(ii) perpendicular to the line.

4 A straight line, **L**, passes through the points $(2, 3)$ and $(4, 9)$.
(a) Work out the equation of the line **L**.
A second straight line, **M**, is perpendicular to **L** and passes through the point with coordinates $(0, -2)$.
(b) Find the equation of this second straight line.

5 The equation of a straight line is $5y + 3x = 15$.
(a) Find:
   (i) the gradient of this line,
   (ii) the coordinates of the point at which the line intercepts the y-axis.

A second straight line is parallel to $5y + 3x = 15$ and passes through the point with coordinates $(-10, 2)$.
(b) Work out the equation of this second straight line.
A third straight line is perpendicular to $5y + 3x = 15$ and passes through the point with coordinates $(12, -1)$.
(c) Find the equation of this third straight line.

6 A straight line passes through the points A and B. The coordinates of A and B are $(2, 3)$ and $(4, -7)$ respectively.
A straight line, **L**, is perpendicular to AB and passes through the point $(0, -3)$.
Find the equation of the line **L**.

3.2 Applying transformations to graphs

- A function is a rule which changes one number into another number.

- f(x), which denotes the output, is read as 'f of x'.

- The graph of $y = x^2 + a$ is the graph of $y = x^2$ translated a units vertically in the **positive** y direction if $a > 0$
  negative y direction if $a < 0$.

- The graph of $y = x + a$ is the graph of $y = x$ translated a units vertically in the **positive** y direction if $a > 0$
  negative y direction if $a < 0$.

- The graph of $y = x^3 + a$ is the graph of $y = x^3$ translated a units vertically in the **positive** y direction if $a > 0$
  negative y direction if $a < 0$.

- The graph of $y = \dfrac{1}{x} + a$ is the graph of $y = \dfrac{1}{x}$ translated a units vertically in the **positive** y direction if $a > 0$
  negative y direction if $a < 0$.

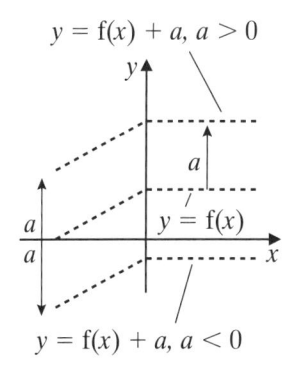

- For any function f, the graph of $y = \text{f}(x) + a$ is the graph of $y = \text{f}(x)$ translated a units vertically in the
  positive y direction if $a > 0$
  negative y direction if $a < 0$.

28 Straight line and transformed graphs

- The graph of $y = (x + a)^2$ is the graph of $y = x^2$ translated a units horizontally in the
  negative x direction if $a > 0$
  positive x direction if $a < 0$.

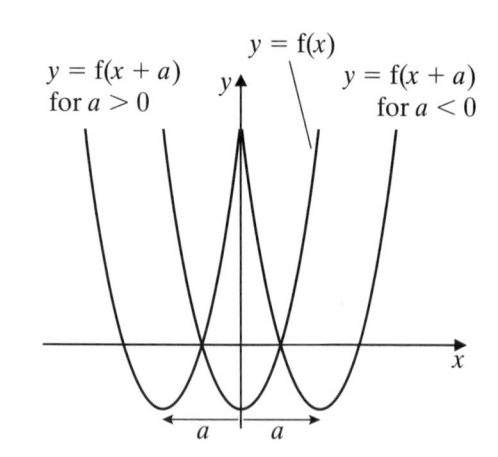

- The vertex of the parabola $y = (x + a)^2$ is at the point $(-a, 0)$.

- To sketch the graph of $y = x^2 + bx + c$, complete the square and apply a double translation to the parabola $y = x^2$.

- The graph of $y = f(x + a) + b$ is the graph of $y = f(x)$ translated a units horizontally
  (in the **negative** x direction if $a > 0$)
  (in the **positive** x direction if $a < 0$)
  and then translated b units vertically (**upwards** if $b > 0$)
  (**downwards** if $b < 0$).

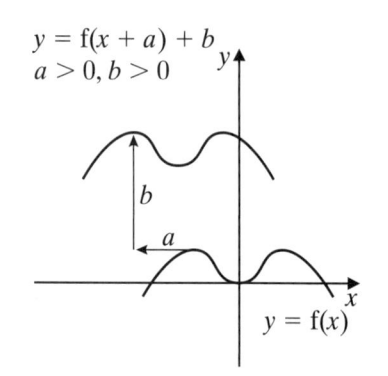

- For any function f, the graph of $y = -f(x)$ is obtained by reflecting $y = f(x)$ in the x-axis.

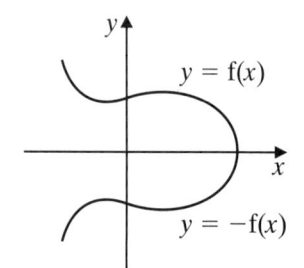

- For any function f, the graph of $y = f(-x)$ is obtained by reflecting $y = f(x)$ in the y-axis.

- Functions f which satisfy $f(-x) = f(x)$ are called *even functions*.

- Functions f which satisfy $f(-x) = -f(x)$ are called *odd functions*.

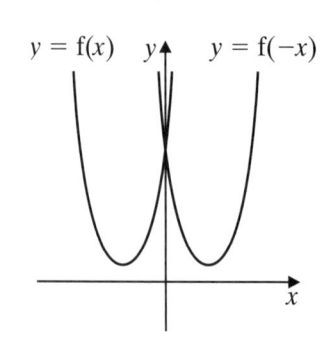

- **For any function f, the graph of $y = af(x)$, where a is a positive constant, is obtained from $y = f(x)$ by applying a stretch of scale factor a parallel to the y-axis.**

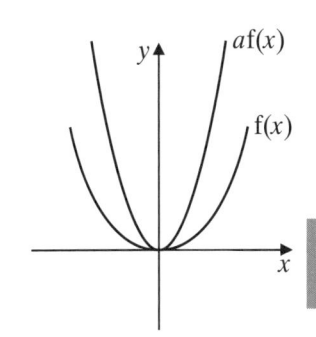

- **For any function f, the graph of $y = f(ax)$, where a is a positive constant, is obtained from $y = f(x)$ by applying a stretch of scale factor $\dfrac{1}{a}$ parallel to the x-axis.**

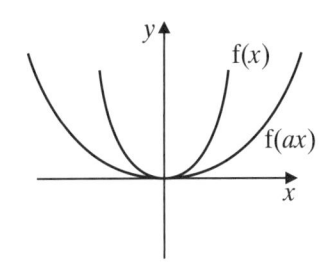

Example 2
The graph of $y = f(x)$ is sketched below:

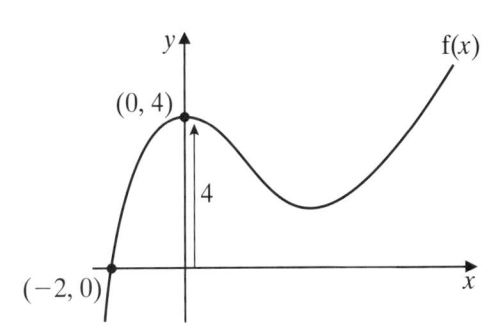

(a) Sketch the graph of $y = f(x - 2)$.
(b) Sketch the graph of $y = f(x) + 3$.
$y = f(x)$ is transformed to $y = g(x)$:

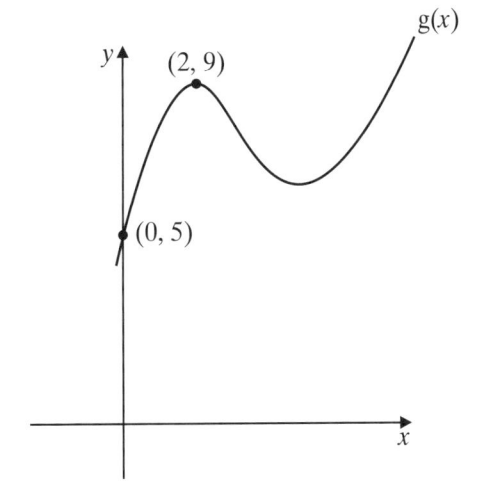

(c) State fully the single transformation which transforms $f(x)$ to $g(x)$.

30 Straight line and transformed graphs

(a) f(x − 2) is as shown:

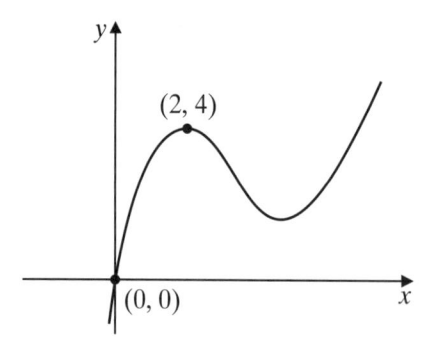

Graph showing curve with points (2, 4) and (0, 0)

(b) f(x) + 3 is as shown:

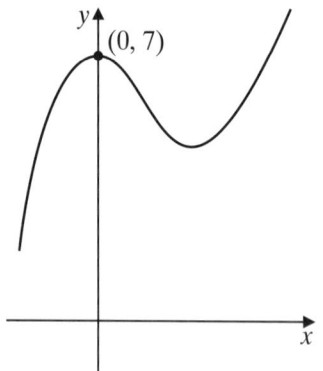

Graph showing curve with point (0, 7)

(c) The single transformation is a translation along the vector $\begin{pmatrix} 2 \\ 5 \end{pmatrix}$.

Example 3

The equation of a curve is

$$y = x^2 - 6x + 11$$

Sketch the graph of y against x.

By completing the square: $y = (x - 3)^2 - 9 + 11$

$$y = (x - 3)^2 + 2$$

So the sketch is:

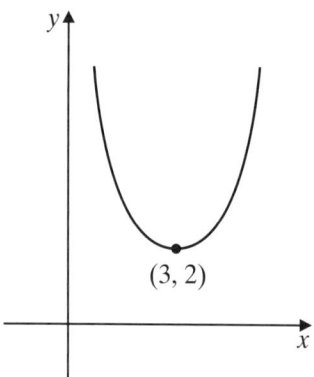

Parabola with minimum at (3, 2)

i.e. $y = x^2$ translated along the vector $\begin{pmatrix} 3 \\ 2 \end{pmatrix}$.

Example 4

The graph of

$y = \sin x°$

for values of x from $0°$ to $360°$ is sketched in the diagram right:

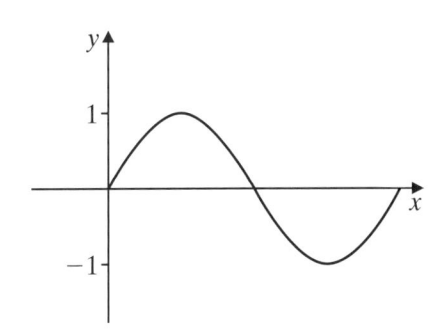

(a) On the same diagram, sketch the graph of

$y = 2\sin(x-30)°$.

The sketch is as shown:

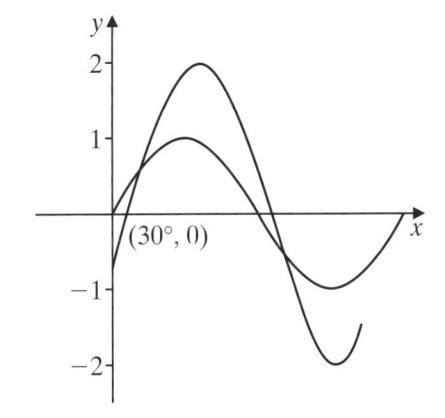

(b) Draw the curve $y = \sin x$, then on the same axes sketch the graph of

$y = \sin 3x$.

The sketch is as shown:

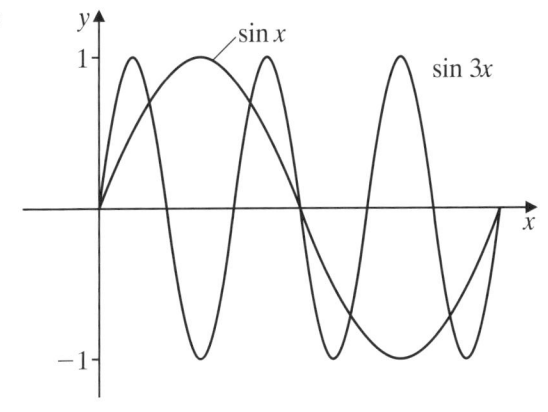

Exercise 3B

1 The equation of a curve is $y = f(x)$, where

$f(x) = x^2 + 8x + 11$

(a) Sketch the graph of $y = f(x)$.
(b) Obtain the minimum value of y and the value of x for which y is a minimum.

The graph of $y = g(x)$ is obtained by reflecting $y = f(x)$ in the x-axis.

(c) Express $g(x)$ as a quadratic in x.

32 Straight line and transformed graphs

2   (a) Sketch the graph of $y = \cos x°$ for values of x from $0°$ to $180°$.
    (b) On the same axes, sketch the graph of $y = 3 \cos(x + 60)°$.
    (c) On the same axes, sketch the graph of $y = \cos 2x$.

3   (a) Sketch the graph of
$$y = 13 - 6x - x^2$$
    (b) Find the maximum value of $13 - 6x - x^2$.
    The graph of $y = g(x)$ is obtained by reflecting $y = 13 - 6x - x^2$ in the line $x = 1$.
    (c) Obtain $g(x)$ in terms of x.

4   Here is the sketch of the curve with equation $y = f(x)$:

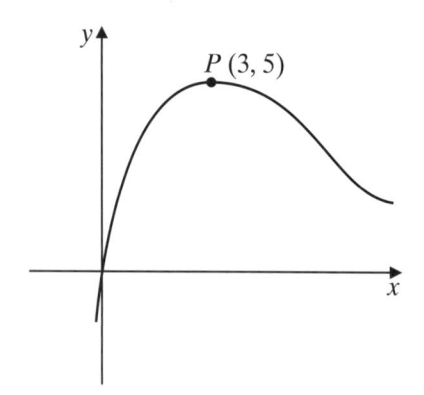

The curve has its only maximum point at the point P with coordinates $(3, 5)$.
Write down the coordinates of the maximum point for curves with each of these equations:

(a) $y = f(x + 1)$ (b) $y = f(x - 3)$ (c) $y = f(x) + 2$
(d) $y = f(-x)$ (e) $y = f(2x)$

5   This is a sketch of the graph of $y = \sin x°$ for values of x between 0 and 360.

    (a) Write down the coordinates of the points
        (i) A,   (ii) B.
    (b) On the same axes sketch the graph of $y = \sin 2x°$ for values of x between 0 and 360.   [E]

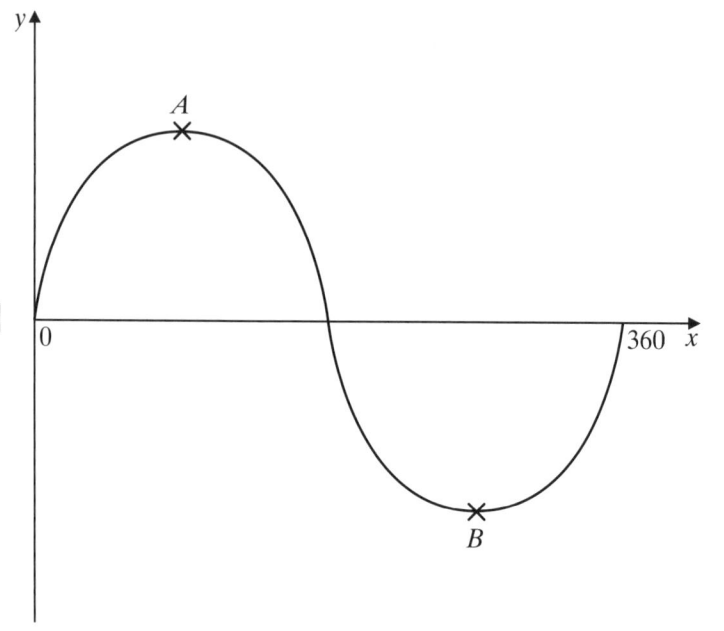

6 The graph of $y = f(x)$ is sketched in the diagrams below.

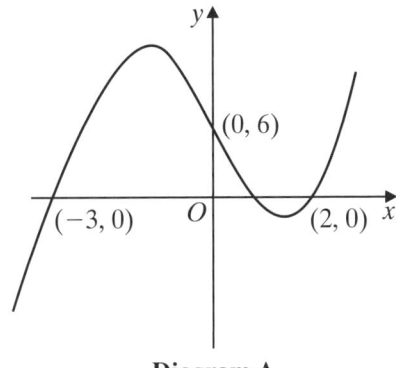

Diagram A

(a) On **Diagram A** sketch the graph of $y = f(x - 3)$.

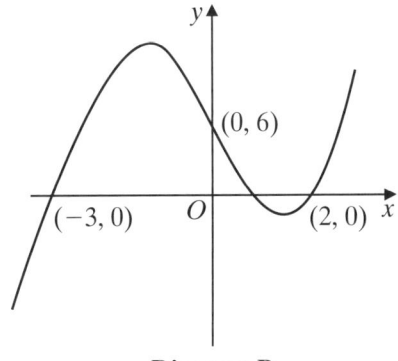

Diagram B

(b) On **Diagram B** sketch the graph of $y = f(x) - 4$. [E]

Exercise 3C Mixed questions

1

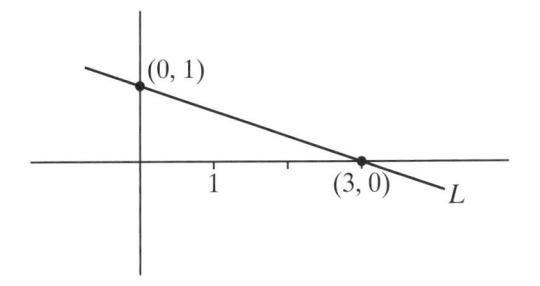

The line L passes through the points $(0, 1)$ and $(3, 0)$.
A line M is perpendicular to L and passes through the point $(3, 3)$.
Find the equation of line M.

2 The equation of a curve is

$$y = x^2 - 8x + 22.$$

(a) Sketch the curve.
(b) Find the minimum value of y.
(c) State the value of x for which y is a minimum.

3 The graph $y = f(x)$ is shown below.

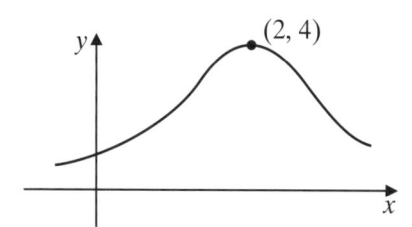

It has a maximum at (2, 4). Write down the coordinates of the maximum point on the curve:

(a) $y = f(x) + 3$
(b) $y = f(x + 3)$
(c) $y = f(2x)$
(d) $y = 2f(x)$

Summary of key points

- An intercept is a point at which a line cuts the y-axis or the x-axis.
- The general form of the equation of a straight line is

    $y = mx + c$

    where m is the gradient and $(0, c)$ is the intercept on the y-axis.
- Lines of the same gradient (m) are parallel.
- If a line has a gradient of m, a line perpendicular to it has a gradient of $\dfrac{-1}{m}$.
- If two lines are perpendicular, the product of their gradients is -1.
- A function is a rule which changes one number into another number.
- $f(x)$, which denotes the output, is read as 'f of x'.
- The graph of $y = x^2 + a$ is the graph of $y = x^2$ translated a units vertically in the **positive** y direction if $a > 0$
  negative y direction if $a < 0$.
- The graph of $y = x + a$ is the graph of $y = x$ translated a units vertically in the **positive** y direction if $a > 0$
  negative y direction if $a < 0$.

- The graph of $y = x^3 + a$ is the graph of $y = x^3$ translated a units vertically in the **positive** y direction if $a > 0$
  negative y direction if $a < 0$.

- The graph of $y = \dfrac{1}{x} + a$ is the graph of $y = \dfrac{1}{x}$ translated a units vertically in the **positive** y direction if $a > 0$
  negative y direction if $a < 0$.

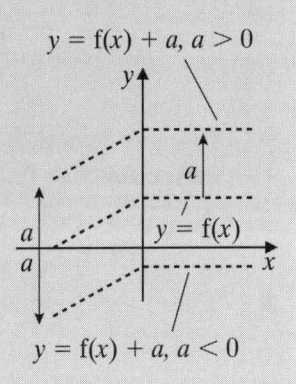

- For any function f, the graph of $y = f(x) + a$ is the graph of $y = f(x)$ translated a units vertically in the
  positive y direction if $a > 0$
  negative y direction if $a < 0$.

- The graph of $y = (x + a)^2$ is the graph of $y = x^2$ translated a units horizontally in the
  negative x direction if $a > 0$
  positive x direction if $a < 0$.

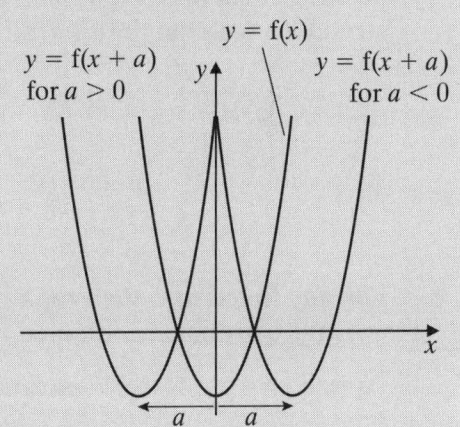

- The vertex of the parabola $y = (x + a)^2$ is at the point $(-a, 0)$.

- To sketch the graph of $y = x^2 + bx + c$, complete the square and apply a double translation to the parabola $y = x^2$.

- The graph of $y = f(x + a) + b$ is the graph of $y = f(x)$ translated a units horizontally
  (in the **negative** x direction if $a > 0$)
  (in the **positive** x direction if $a < 0$)
  and then translated b units vertically (**upwards** if $b > 0$)
  (**downwards** if $b < 0$).

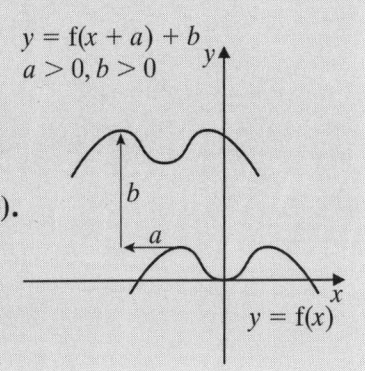

- For any function f, the graph of $y = -f(x)$ is obtained by reflecting $y = f(x)$ in the x-axis.

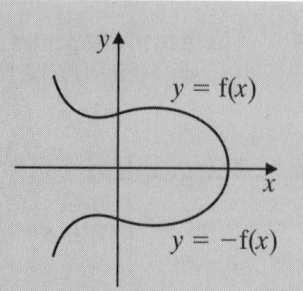

- For any function f, the graph of $y = f(-x)$ is obtained by reflecting $y = f(x)$ in the y-axis.

- Functions f which satisfy $f(-x) = f(x)$ are called *even functions*.

- Functions f which satisfy $f(-x) = -f(x)$ are called *odd functions*.

- For any function f, the graph of $y = af(x)$, where a is a positive constant, is obtained from $y = f(x)$ by applying a stretch of scale factor a parallel to the y-axis.

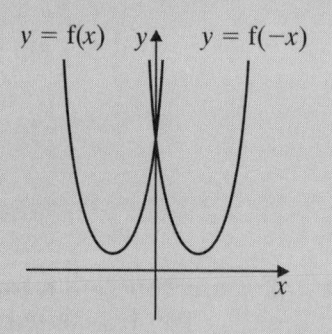

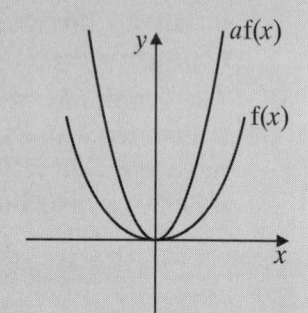

- For any function f, the graph of $y = f(ax)$, where a is a positive constant, is obtained from $y = f(x)$ by applying a stretch of scale factor $\dfrac{1}{a}$ parallel to the x-axis.

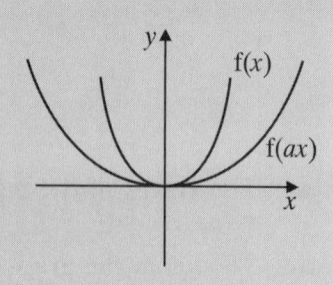

4 Trigonometric functions

4.1 The sine rule

Teaching reference:
pp 457–461, section 22.2

- In any triangle, including right-angled triangles,

$$\frac{a}{\sin A} = \frac{b}{\sin B} = \frac{c}{\sin C}$$

or

$$\frac{\sin A}{a} = \frac{\sin B}{b} = \frac{\sin C}{c}$$

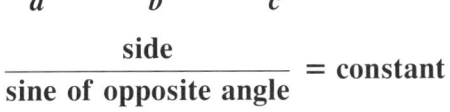

$$\frac{\text{side}}{\text{sine of opposite angle}} = \text{constant}$$

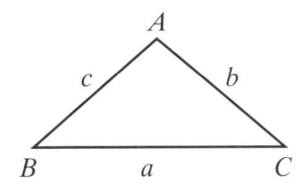

- $\sin x = \sin (180 - x)$

Example 1
Find BC:

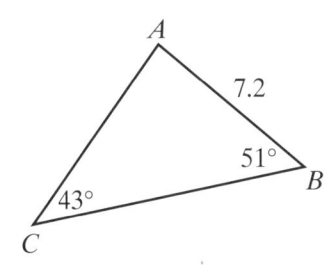

Angle $A = 180 - 43 - 51 = 86°$

$$\therefore \frac{7.2}{\sin 43} = \frac{BC}{\sin 86}$$

$$BC = \frac{7.2 \sin 86}{\sin 43} = 10.53 \quad (2 \text{ d.p.})$$

Exercise 4A   Links (22C) 22C

In each question, work out the value of the marked letter.

1. (triangle: 15, 53°, 27°, a)
2. (triangle: 41°, 23, 47°, b)
3. (triangle: c, 31°, 7.2, 102°)
4. (triangle: 8.7, 37°, 51°, d)

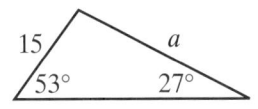

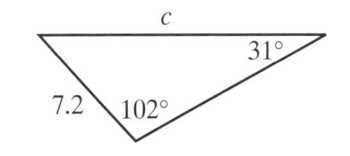

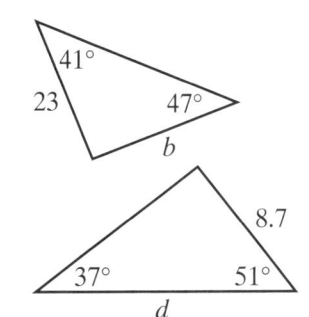

38 Trigonometric functions

5
14°, 23°, 9.2, e

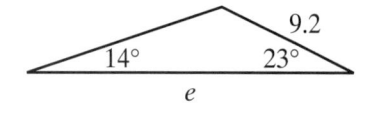

6
15.3, 5.7, 47°, A 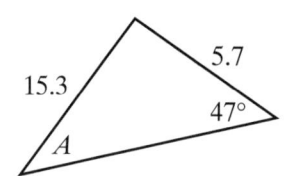

7
6.2, B, 5.1, 75°

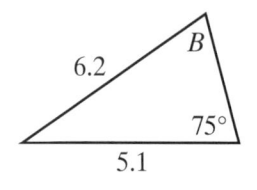

8
8.3, 40°, 7.2, C

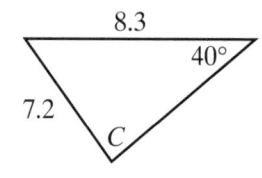

(This question has two possible answers.)

4.2 The cosine rule

Teaching reference: pp 461–464, section 22.3

- $a^2 = b^2 + c^2 - 2bc \cos A$

  or $\cos A = \dfrac{b^2 + c^2 - a^2}{2bc}$

- $\cos x = -\cos (180 - x)$

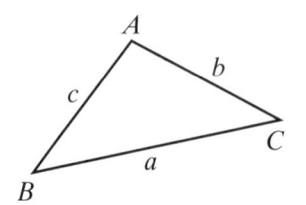

Example 2

In the diagram, work out
(a) BC and (b) angle B.

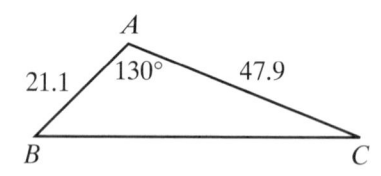

(Triangle with A at top, angle 130°, $AB = 21.1$, $AC = 47.9$)

(a) $BC^2 = (21.1^2) + (47.9^2) - 2(21.1)(47.9) \cos 130°$

$= 445.21 + 2294.41 - 2021.38 \cos 130°$

$= 2739.62 - (-1299.318)$

$= 4038.938$

$BC = 63.55$ to 2 d.p.

It is essential to do the operations in the correct order.

(b) Now, using the sine rule:

$\dfrac{\sin 130}{63.55} = \dfrac{\sin B}{47.9}$

$\sin B = \dfrac{47.9 \sin 130}{63.55} = 0.577\,372\,2$

angle $B = 35.3°$ (1 d.p.)

Exercise 4B   Links (*22E*) 22E

In each question, work out the third side and the other angles.

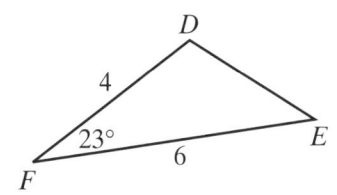

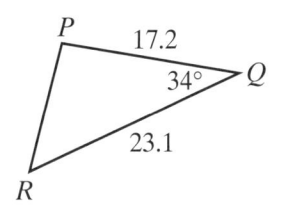

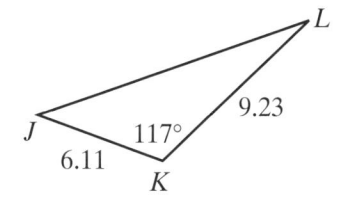

1 Triangle with $CA = 15$, $AB = 8$, angle $A = 120°$.

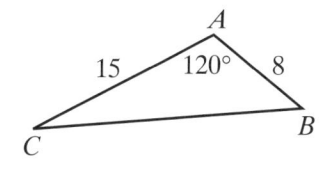

2 Triangle with $FD = 4$, $FE = 6$, angle $F = 23°$.

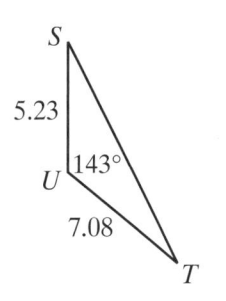

3 Triangle with $PQ = 17.2$, $PR = 23.1$, angle $P = 34°$.

4 Triangle with $JK = 6.11$, $KL = 9.23$, angle $K = 117°$.

5 Triangle with $SU = 5.23$, $UT = 7.08$, angle $U = 143°$.

6 Triangle with $ZX = 8.81$, $XY = 6.73$, angle $X = 11.3°$.

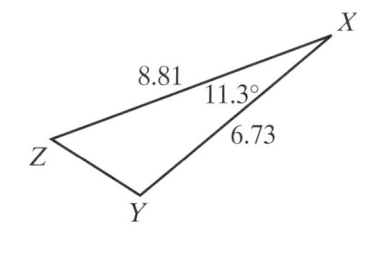

Example 3
Find the angles in the triangle:

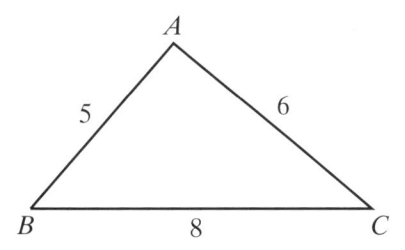

Triangle ABC with $AB = 5$, $AC = 6$, $BC = 8$.

The smallest angle is opposite the smallest side.
It must be acute.

$$\cos C = \frac{8^2 + 6^2 - 5^2}{2 \times 8 \times 6} = 0.781\,25$$

angle $C = 38.6°$ to 1 d.p.

$$\cos A = \frac{6^2 + 5^2 - 8^2}{2 \times 6 \times 5} = -0.05$$

angle $A = 92.9°$ to 1 d.p.

angle $B = 180 -$ angle $A -$ angle C
$\qquad = 48.5°$ to 1 d.p.

Exercise 4C Links (22E) 22E

In questions **1–4**, work out the sizes of the angles in the triangle.

1 Triangle ABC with $CA = 7$, $AB = 4$, $CB = 8$.

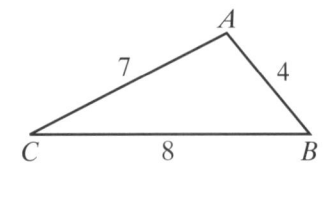

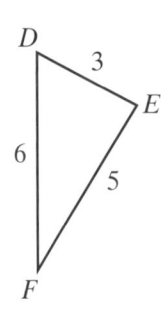

2 Triangle DEF with $DE = 3$, $EF = 5$, $DF = 6$.

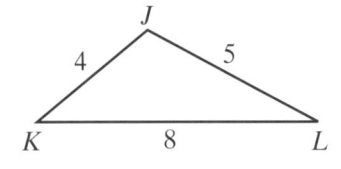

3 Triangle JKL with $KJ = 4$, $JL = 5$, $KL = 8$.

4 Triangle PQR with $PR = 6.13$, $PQ = 10.08$, $RQ = 5.29$.

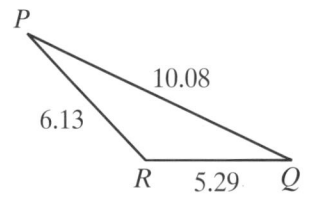

5

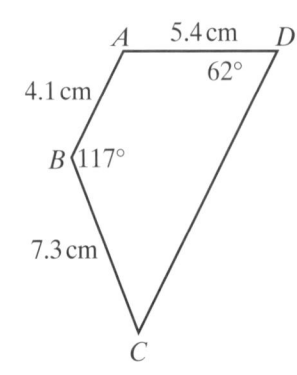

The diagram shows a quadrilateral $ABCD$.
$AB = 4.1\,\text{cm}$
$BC = 7.3\,\text{cm}$
$AD = 5.4\,\text{cm}$
Angle $ABC = 117°$
Angle $ADC = 62°$

Remember the formula for the area of a triangle:
$$\text{area} = \tfrac{1}{2}ab\sin C$$

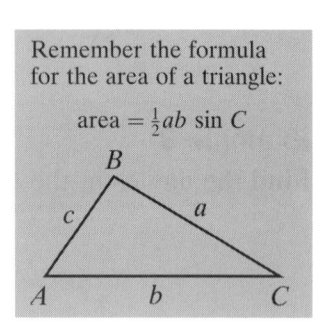

(a) Calculate the length of AC.
    Give your answer correct to 3 significant figures.
(b) Calculate the area of triangle ABC.
(c) Calculate the area of quadrilateral $ABCD$. [E]

6 Triangle with $CA = 8\,\text{cm}$, $CB = 10\,\text{cm}$, angle $ACB = 80°$.

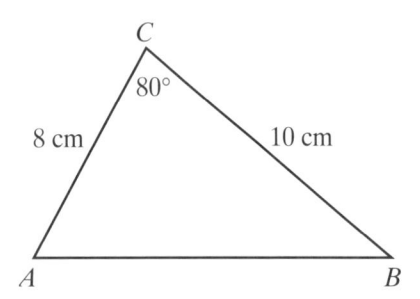

(a) Calculate the length of AB.
    Give your answer correct to 3 significant figures.
(b) Calculate the size of angle ABC.
    Give your answer correct to 3 significant figures. [E]

7   A plane flies on a bearing of 037° for 200 km before changing to a heading of 083° for a distance of 300 km.
    Calculate its distance and bearing from its starting point.

8   A ship sailing on a bearing of 140° first sights lighthouse L at 1100 hours on a bearing of 080°. It is known to be 24 km away. Three hours later the ship, now at B, sees the same lighthouse at a distance of 40 km.
   (a) Work out the ship's average speed.
   (b) M is the closest the ship gets to the lighthouse. Work out the distance LM.

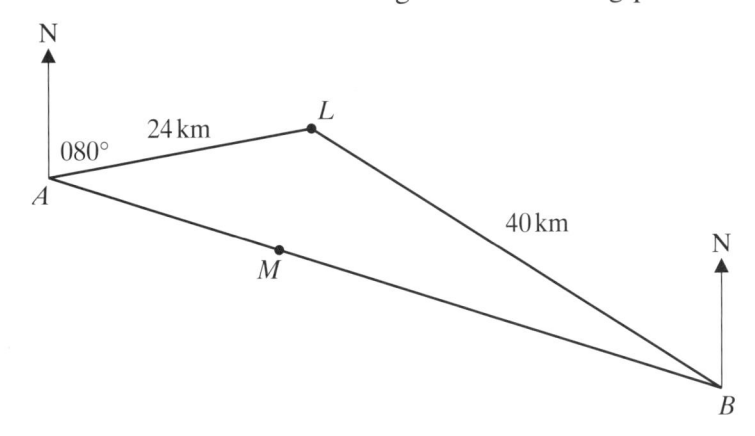

4.3 Graphs of trigonometric functions

Teaching reference:
pp 283–289, 502–503,
sections 13.6, 13.7, 13.8, 24.7

■ The graph of $y = \sin x$ is:

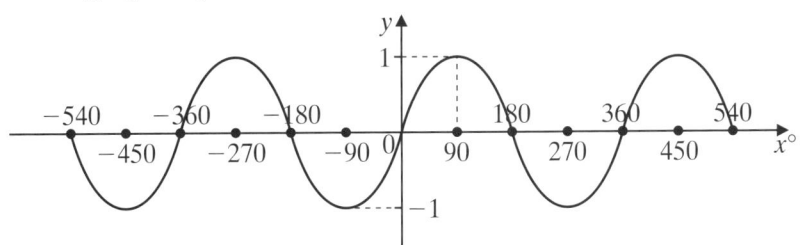

■ The graph of $y = \cos x$ is:

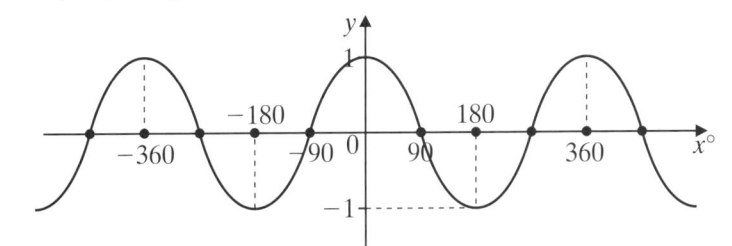

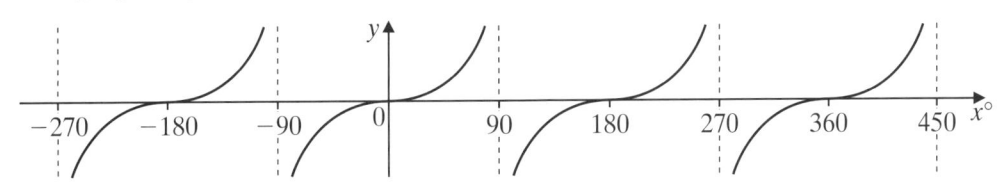

■ The graph of $y = \tan x$ is:

Example 4

Sketch the graph of $y = 2 \sin x$.

The maximum and minimum values of $\sin x$ are $+1$ and -1.
For $2 \sin x$ the maximum and minimum values are $+2$ and -2.
The intercepts on the x-axis are unchanged.
This means that the function $2 \sin x$ stretches the function $\sin x$ in the y direction with a scale factor of 2. Its sketch looks like this:

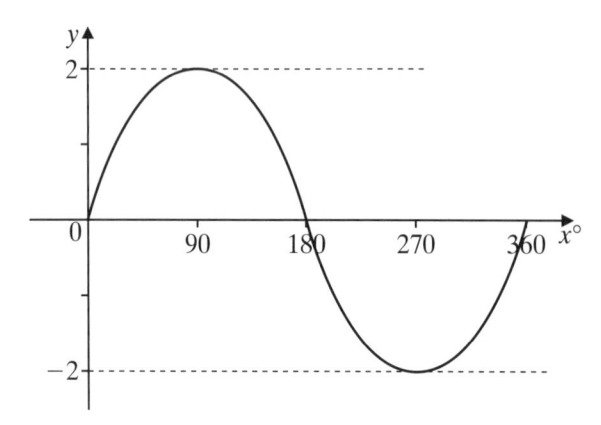

Example 5

Sketch the graph of $y = \sin 2x$.

$\sin 2x$ has the same maximum and minimum as $\sin x$.
In the x direction, $\sin 2x$ completes a complete cycle in $180°$ instead of $360°$.

The function $\sin 2x$ is a stretch of the function $\sin x$ in the x direction with a scale factor of $\frac{1}{2}$.

The sketch of $y = \sin 2x$ looks like this:

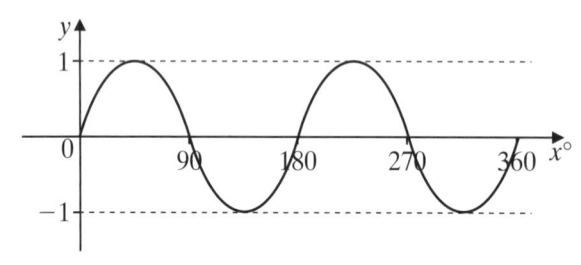

Similar results can be deduced for cosine and tangent functions.

Exercise 4D   Links (*13H, 24I*) 13H, 24I

Draw sketches for x from -360 to $+360$ for the following functions.

1	$4 \sin x$	**2**	$3 \tan x$	**3**	$2 \cos x$	**4**	$-2 \sin x$
5	$-\tan x$	**6**	$-3 \sin x$	**7**	$\cos 2x$	**8**	$\sin \frac{1}{2} x$
9	$2 \sin 3x$	**10**	$5 \cos 2x$				

4.4 Solving simple trigonometric equations

Teaching reference: pp 287–288, section 13.8

The following results can be seen from the symmetrical features of trigonometric graphs:

$\sin(-x) = -\sin x$
$\sin(180 - x) = \sin x$
$\sin(360 + x) = \sin x$

$\cos(-x) = \cos x$
$\cos(180 - x) = -\cos x$
$\cos(360 + x) = \cos x$

$\tan(-x) = -\tan x$
$\tan(180 - x) = -\tan x$
$\tan(360 + x) = \tan x$

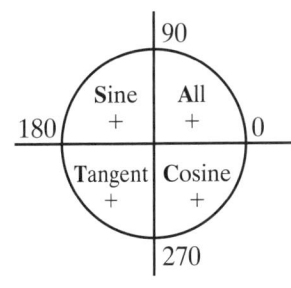

The ACTS diagram shows when the trigonometric functions are positive.

Example 6

Solve the equation $5 \sin 3x - 3 = 0$ for $0° \leqslant x \leqslant 180°$.

$5 \sin 3x = 3$
$\sin 3x = \frac{3}{5} = 0.6$

Hence $3x = 36.9$ or 143.1 or 396.9 or 503.1 etc.
$x = 12.3, 47.7, 132.3, 167.7.$ (All to 1 d.p.)

Use the results quoted above to find the other possible values of $3x$.

Exercise 4E
Links (13I) 13I

1. For values of x in the range $0°$ to $360°$, solve $4 \sin x = 1$.
2. For values of x in the range $0°$ to $360°$, solve $2 \tan x = 3$.
3. For values of x in the range $0°$ to $360°$, solve $2 \cos 2x = 1$.
4. For values of x in the range $0°$ to $180°$, solve $5 \cos 2x = 2$.
5. For values of x in the range $0°$ to $720°$, solve $2 \tan 3x = 10$.
6. For values of x from $-180°$ to $180°$, solve $3 \sin x + 1 = 0$.
7. For values of x in the range $-180°$ to $180°$, solve $5 \sin 2x + 1 = 0$.
8. For values of x in the range $-180°$ to $180°$, solve $4 \tan 2x + 6 = 0$.

4.5 Angles between a line and a plane

Teaching reference: pp 465–467, section 22.4

To find the angle between a line and a plane, you need to draw a perpendicular from a point on the line down to the plane. This makes a right angle to work with.

Example 7

In the shape below, A is 1 m horizontally from M, the mid-point of PQ. Find the angle AQ makes with the horizontal.

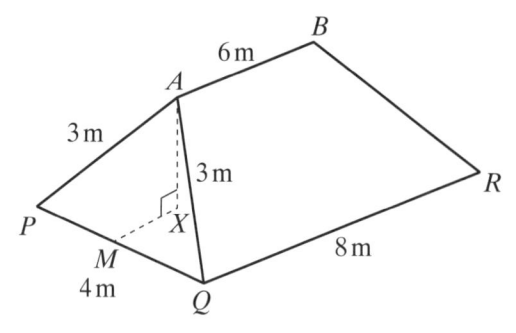

A separate diagram often helps:

In triangle XMQ, $MQ = 2$, $MX = 1$, angle $XMQ = 90°$.

Therefore by Pythagoras $XQ^2 = (2^2 + 1^2) = 5$
$$XQ = \sqrt{5}$$

In triangle AXQ, angle AXQ is $90°$.

Therefore $\cos AQX = \dfrac{\sqrt{5}}{3}$

angle $AQX = 41.8°$ (1 d.p.)

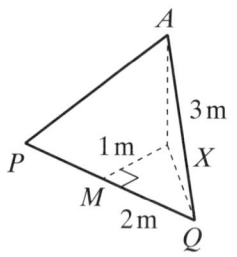

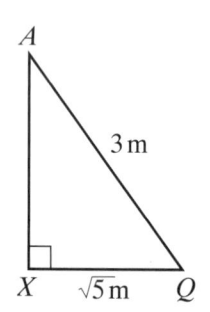

Exercise 4F   Links (22G) 22G

1. By travelling diagonally across the road the steepness is reduced.
   Work out the angle AB makes with the horizontal.

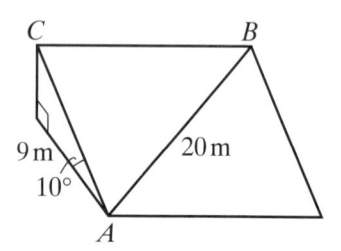

2. This shape is a square-based pyramid.
   Work out the angle an edge makes with the horizontal face.

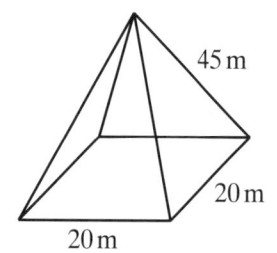

3 A vertical flagpole stands at the corner of a rectangular parade ground.
Work out the angle of elevation of the top of the flagpole from the corner *P*.

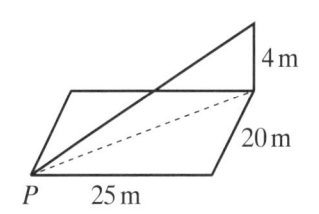

Exercise 4G — Mixed questions

1

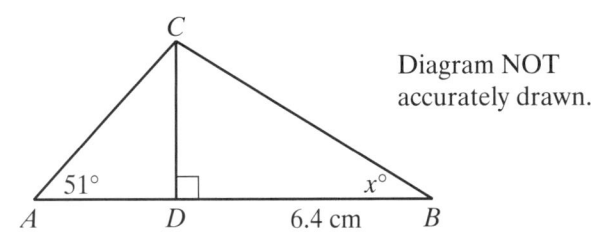

The diagram shows a triangle *ABC*.
The line *CD* is perpendicular to the line *AB*.
$AC = 7.3$ cm, $BD = 6.4$ cm and angle $BAC = 51°$.

Calculate the size of the angle marked $x°$.
Give your answer correct to 1 decimal place. (E)

2

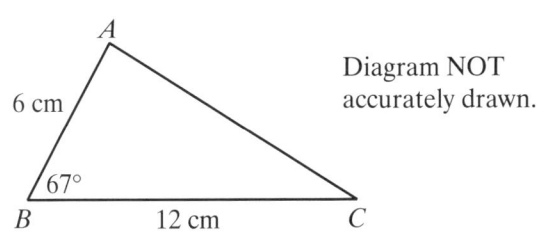

Diagram NOT accurately drawn.

The diagram shows a triangle *ABC*.
$AB = 6$ cm, $BC = 12$ cm, angle $B = 67°$.

Calculate the length *AC*.
Give your answer correct to 3 significant figures. (E)

3

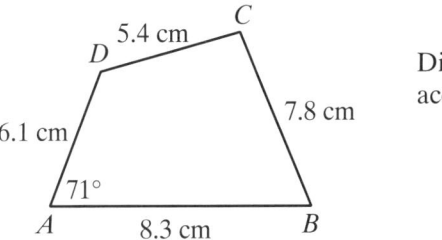

Diagram NOT accurately drawn.

The diagram shows a quadrilateral *ABCD*.
$AB = 8.3$ cm, $BC = 7.8$ cm, $CD = 5.4$ cm and $AD = 6.1$ cm
Angle $BAD = 71°$

(a) Calculate the area of triangle *ABD*.
   Give your answer correct to 3 significant figures.
(b) Calculate the size of angle *BCD*.
   Give your answer correct to 1 decimal place. (E)

46 Trigonometric functions

4 A tower is 92 metres high.
From the top of the tower, point A is on a bearing of 063° with an angle of depression of 53°.
From the same point at the top of the tower, point B is on a bearing of 140° with an angle of depression of 71°.
Calculate the distance AB.

5 A motorway runs in a north-easterly direction (its bearing is 045°).
Peter is 200 m due east of a point on the motorway.
He sees a kestrel hovering above the motorway on a bearing of 020°.
The angle of elevation of the kestrel is 36°.
Calculate the height of the kestrel.

6 The rise and fall of a tide can be modelled by the function
$$f(t) = 10\cos(30t)° + 25$$
This gives the height in feet when t is the time on the 24 hour clock.
(a) Write down the height of low tide.
(b) Write down the height of high tide.
(c) Work out the number of hours between high and low tide.

7 The depth of water, d metres, at the entrance to a harbour is given by the formula
$$d = 5 - 4\sin(30t)°$$
where t is the time in hours after midnight on one day.
(a) Draw the graph of d against t for $0 < t < 12$
(b) Find two values of t, where $0 < t < 24$, when the depth is least. (E)

8 The diagram shows a sketch of part of the curve
$y = f(x) = \cos x°$

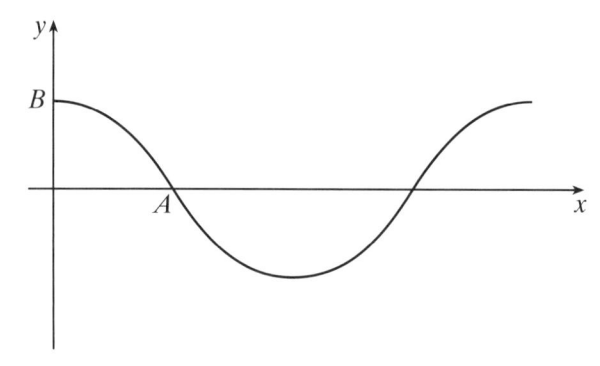

(a) Write down the co-ordinates of the points A and B.
(b) Draw this function and, on the same diagram, sketch the graph of $y = f(2x)$ (E)

Summary of key points

- In any triangle, including right-angled triangles,

$$\frac{a}{\sin A} = \frac{b}{\sin B} = \frac{c}{\sin C}$$

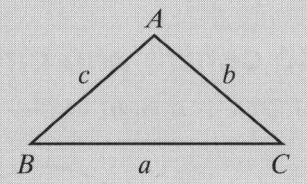

- $\sin x = \sin(180 - x)$
- $a^2 = b^2 + c^2 - 2bc \cos A$

$$\cos A = \frac{b^2 + c^2 - a^2}{2bc}$$

- $\cos x = -\cos(180 - x)$
- The graph of $y = \sin x$ is:

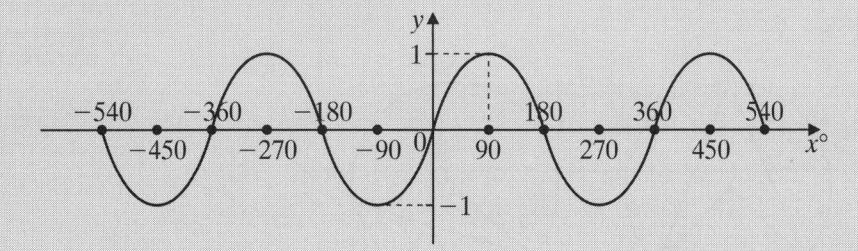

- The graph of $y = \cos x$ is:

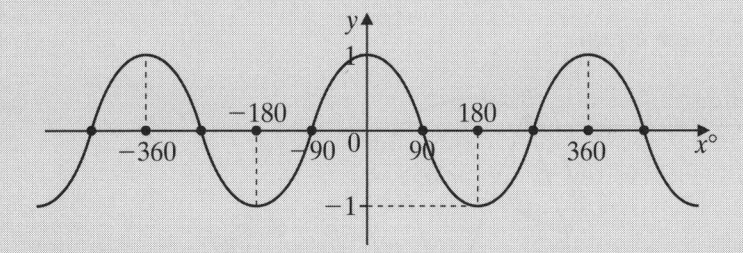

- The graph of $y = \tan x$ is:

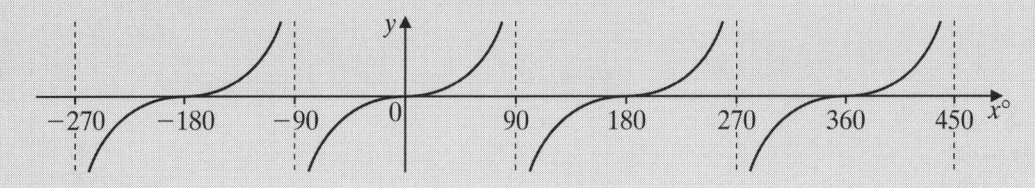

5 Circle theorems

5.1 Angles at the centre and circumference

Teaching reference: pp 528–534, sections 26.2, 26.3, 26.4

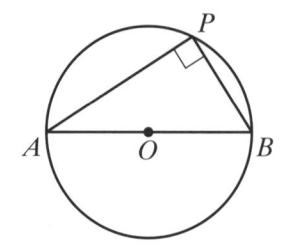

- **The angle in a semicircle is a right angle.**

Angle $APB = 90°$

- **The angle subtended at the centre is twice the angle at the circumference.**

Angle $AOB = 2 \times$ angle APB

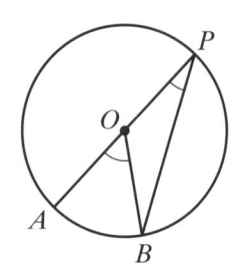

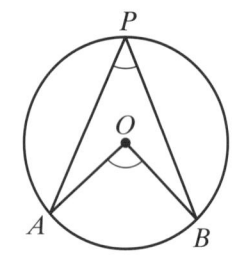

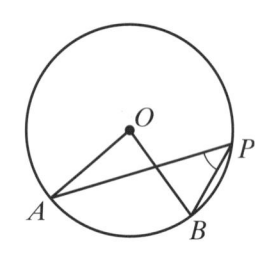

- **Angles in the same segment are equal.**

Angle $APB =$ angle AQB

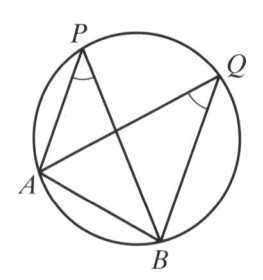

Example 1
Angle $APB = 38°$.
Find angles AQB and AOB.
Give reasons for your answers.

Angle $AQB =$ angle $APB = 38°$ (angles in the same segment)

Angle $AOB = 2 \times$ angle $AQB = 76°$ (angle at centre $= 2 \times$ angle at circumference)

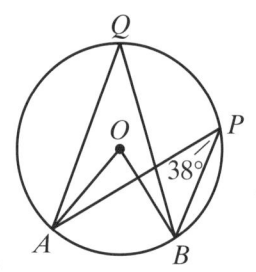

Exercise 5A   Links 26B, 26C, 26D

In each question, work out the named angles.
O, where shown, is the centre of the circle.

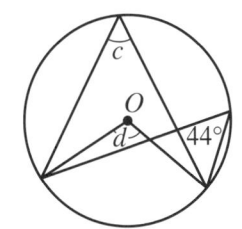

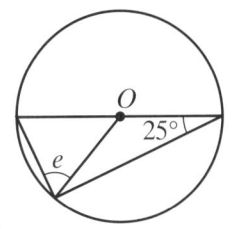

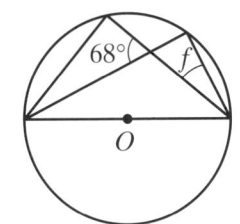

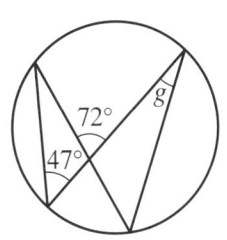

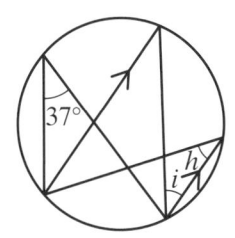

1 $114°$, a, b

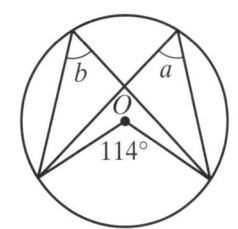

2 c, d, $44°$

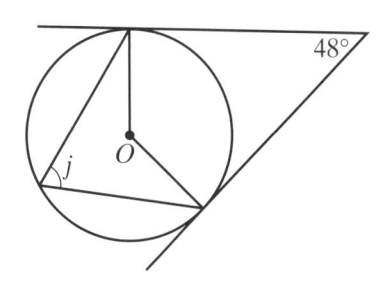

3 $25°$, e

4 $68°$, f

5 $72°$, g, $47°$

6 $37°$, h, i

7 $48°$, j

8 $56°$, k, m

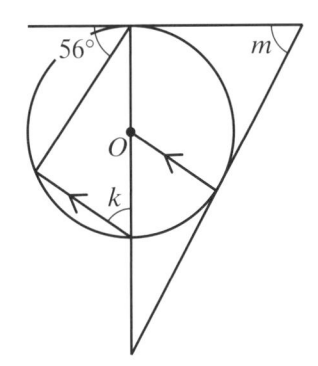

5.2 Cyclic quadrilaterals

- **Opposite angles in a cyclic quadrilateral are supplementary (they add up to $180°$).**

$$\text{Angle } A + \text{angle } C = 180°$$
$$\text{Angle } B + \text{angle } D = 180°$$

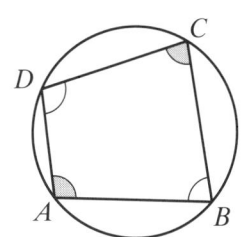

50 Circle theorems

Example 2

OQ is parallel to BP. Angle $QOP = 63°$.
Find angle AXB.
Give reasons for your answer.

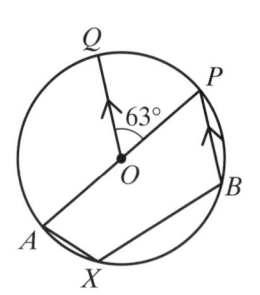

Angle OPB = angle $QOP = 63°$ (alternate angles)

Angle $AXB = 180 -$ angle APB (opposite angles in a
$= 180 - 63 = 117°$ cyclic quadrilateral)

Exercise 5B   Links 26E

1 Find the angles marked a and b.

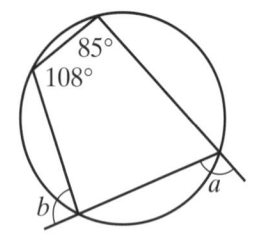

2 $AD = DC$.
Find angle B.

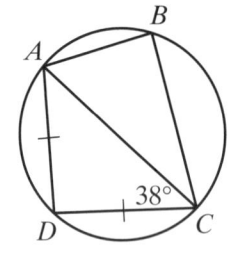

3 $AC = CB$.
Angle $C = 54°$.
Find angle XTY.

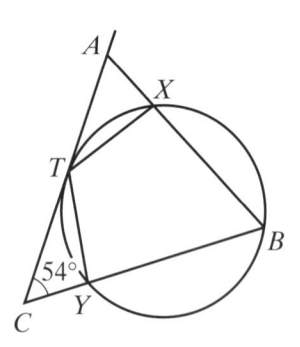

4 PT and PS are tangents.
O is the centre.
Find angle TYS.

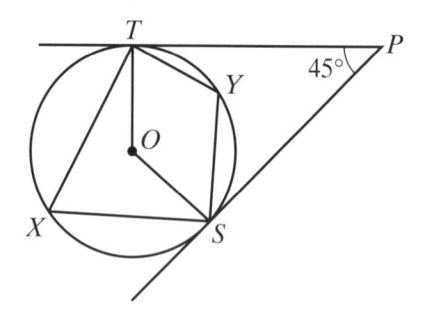

5 Angle $BAC = 26°$.
Angle $BDA = 30°$.
Find angle ABC.

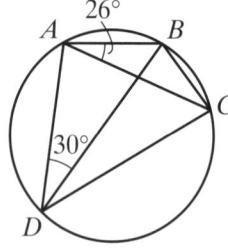

6 Angle $DAC = 42°$.
Angle $ABC = 105°$.
Find angles ADC and ACD.

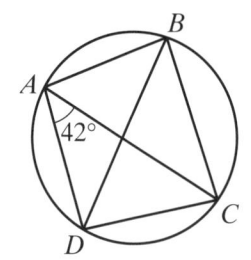

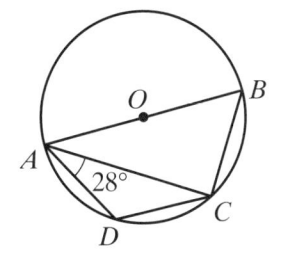

7

AD = DC.
AOB is a diameter.
Find angles ABC and BAC.

8

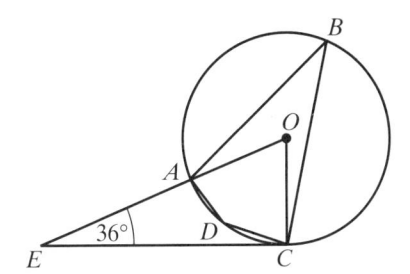

Diagram NOT accurately drawn.

A, B, C and D are points on the circumference of a circle centre O.
A tangent is drawn from E to touch the circle at C.
Angle AEC = 36°.
EAO is a straight line.
(a) Calculate the size of angle ABC.
    Give reasons for your answer.
(b) Calculate the size of angle ADC.
    Give a reason for your answer. (E)

5.3 The alternate segment theorem

■ **The angle between a tangent and its chord is equal to the angle in the alternate segment.**

Angle RQX = angle QYX

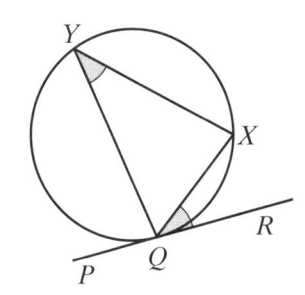

Example 3

Angle $ABC = 73°$.
Angle $CTQ = 40°$.
TQ is a tangent.
Find angle ACT.
Give reasons for your answer.

Angle $CBT = 40°$ (alternate segment)
Angle $ABT = 73 - 40 = 33°$
Angle ACT = angle $ABT = 33°$ (angles in same segment)

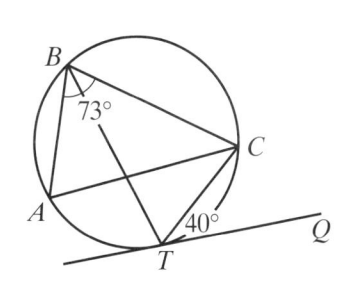

Exercise 5C Links 26F

1 Find angle *TBA*.

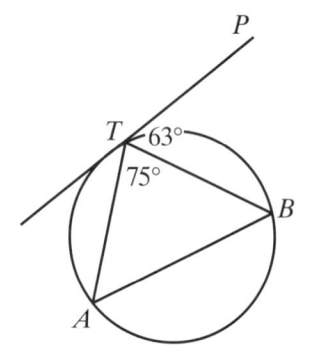

2 Find angles *ABT* and *BTC*.

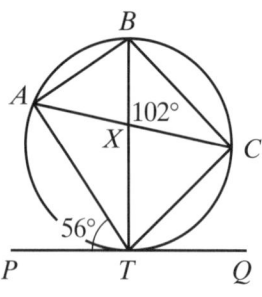

3 *PTQ* is a tangent.
AB = *AT*.
Find angle *ABT*.

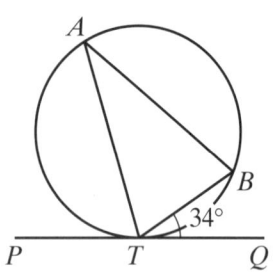

4 *PTQ* is a tangent.
AB is parallel to *ST*.
Find angle *BTA*.

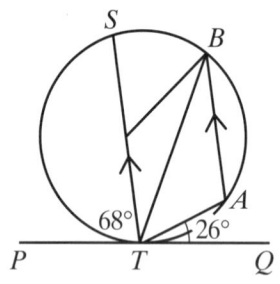

5 *PTQ* is a tangent.
Find angle *CBT*.

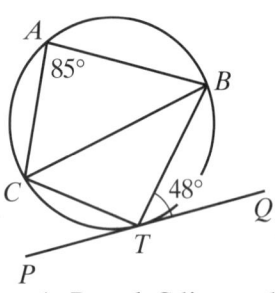

6 Points *A*, *B* and *C* lie on the circumference of a circle with centre *O*.

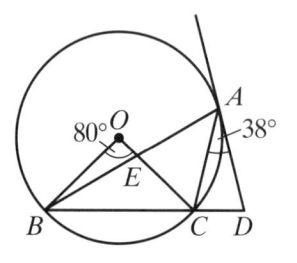

DA is the tangent to the circle at *A*.
BCD is a straight line.
OC and *AB* intersect at *E*.
Angle *BOC* = 80°.
Angle *CAD* = 38°.
(a) Calculate the size of angle *BAC*.
(b) Calculate the size of angle *OBA*.
(c) Give a reason why it is not possible to draw a circle with diameter *ED* through the point *A*. (E)

5.4 Geometrical proof

Example 4
Prove angle $AOB = 2 \times$ angle APB.

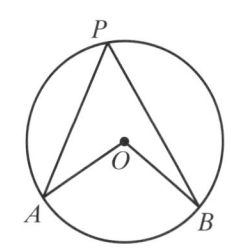

Join PO and extend to Q:

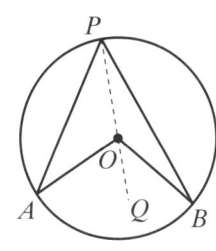

Triangle AOP is isosceles so angle $OAP =$ angle APO.

But angle $OAP +$ angle $APO =$ angle AOQ (exterior angle = sum of interior opposite angles)

so angle $AOQ = 2 \times$ angle APO
Similarly angle $BOQ = 2 \times$ angle BPO
Adding these results:

angle $AOB = 2 \times$ angle APB

This proof works whether angle AOB is acute, obtuse, 180° or reflex.

Example 5
Prove angle $ATP =$ angle TBA
(the alternate segment theorem).

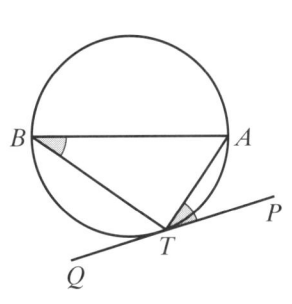

Draw the diameter TX. Join AX.

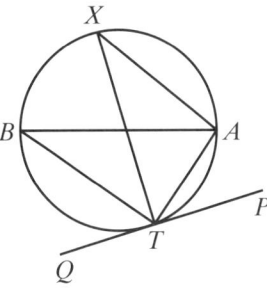

Angle $PTX = 90°$ (tangent is perpendicular to radius at point of contact)

Angle $XAT = 90°$ (angle in a semicircle)

54 Circle theorems

Angle $ATP = 90 -$ angle ATX
Angle $AXT = 180 - 90 -$ angle $ATX = 90 -$ angle ATX

so angle $ATP =$ angle AXT
But angle $AXT =$ angle TBA (angles in the same segment)

So angle $TBA =$ angle ATP

Exercise 5D   Links 26G

1. Prove that triangles BXA and CXD are similar.

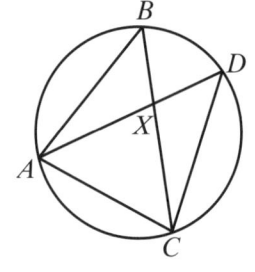

2. AB is parallel to CD.
   Prove that triangle CXD is isosceles.

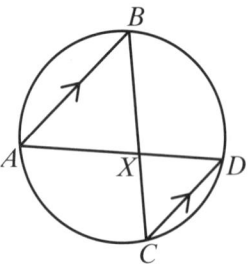

3. PTQ is a tangent.
   Prove PAT and PTB are similar triangles.

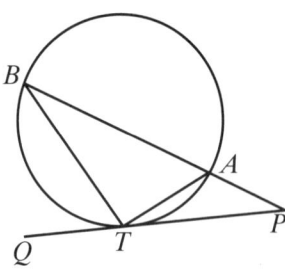

4. PT is a tangent.
   $PA = TA$.
   Prove $PT = TX$.

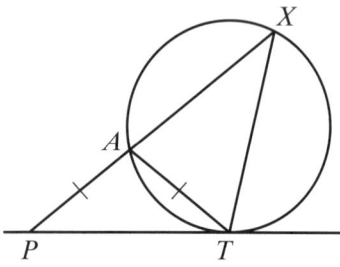

5. Prove triangles APS and AQR are similar.

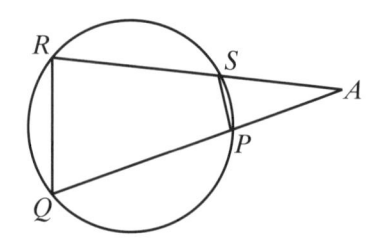

6

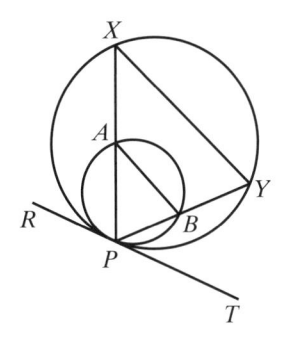

RPT is a tangent to the circles at the point of contact.
PAX and *PBY* are straight lines.
Prove *AB* is parallel to *XY*.

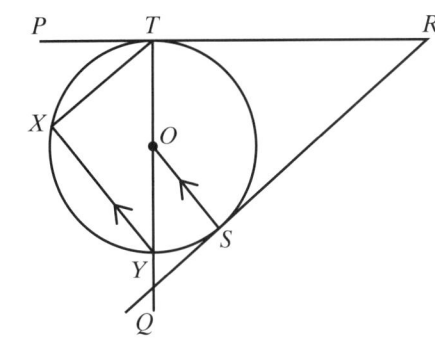

7

PTR and *RSQ* are tangents.
O is the centre.
XY is parallel to *OS*.
Prove triangles *TXY* and *TRQ* are similar.
Hence show *TX* is parallel to *RQ*.

Summary of key points

- **The angle in a semicircle is a right angle.**

Angle $APB = 90°$

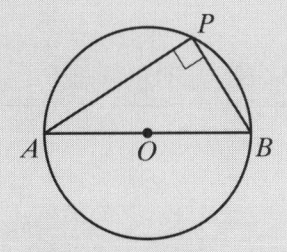

- **The angle subtended at the centre is twice the angle at the circumference.**

Angle $AOB = 2 \times$ angle APB

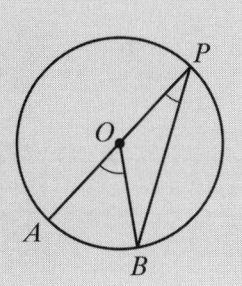

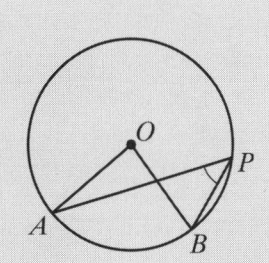

Circle theorems

- **Angles in the same segment are equal.**

    Angle APB = angle AQB

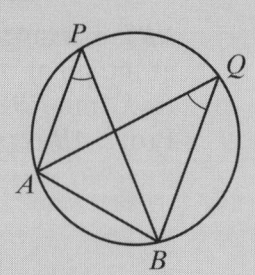

- **Opposite angles in a cyclic quadrilateral are supplementary (they add up to 180°).**

    Angle A + angle $C = 180°$

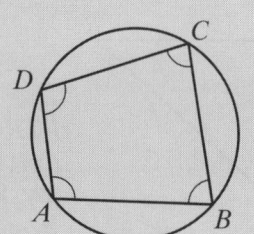

    Angle B + angle $D = 180°$

- **The angle between a tangent and its chord is equal to the angle in the alternate segment.**

    Angle RQX = angle QYX

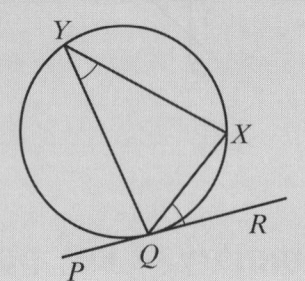

6 Advanced measure and mensuration

6.1 Dimension theory

- $1\,m^2 = 100 \times 100\,cm^2 = 10\,000\,cm^2$

- $1\,m^3 = 100 \times 100 \times 100\,cm^3 = 1\,000\,000\,cm^3$

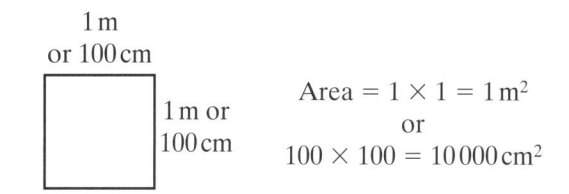

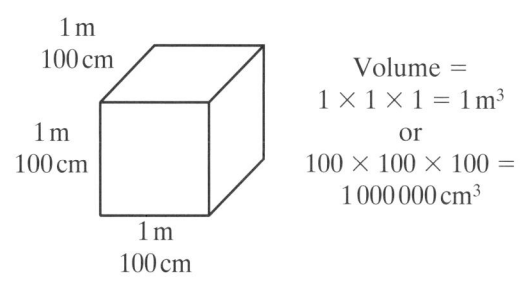

- All formulae for **length** or **distance** have the dimension
  length   and are dimension 1
- All formulae for **area** have the dimensions
  length × length   and are dimension 2
- All formulae for **volume** have the dimensions
  length × length × length   and are dimension 3

Numbers, e.g. 3, $\frac{4}{5}$, π and $\sqrt{2}$, are dimensionless.

Example 1

Here are three expressions related to the circular measure with radius r:

(a) $\frac{2}{3}\pi r^3$ (b) $2\pi r$ (c) πr^2

State whether each expression is a length, area or volume, giving your reasons.

(a) $\frac{2}{3}\pi r^3$

  In this expression $\frac{2}{3}$ and π are numbers so are dimensionless.
  r is a length so r^3 has dimension 3.
  Therefore $\frac{2}{3}\pi r^3$ has dimension 3, so this expression represents a volume.

(b) $2\pi r$

  In this expression 2 and π are numbers so are dimensionless.
  r is a length so r has dimension 1.
  Therefore $2\pi r$ has dimension 1, so this expression represents a length.

58 Advanced measure and mensuration

(c) πr^2
In this expression π is a number so is dimensionless.
r is a length so r^2 has dimension 2.
Therefore πr^2 has dimension 2, so this expression represents an area.

Exercise 6A   Links (*16I*) 16I

1. State whether each of the following expressions is a length, area or volume, giving your reasons.
    (a) $\frac{4}{3}\pi r^3$ (b) $\pi r^2 h$ (c) πd
    (d) $\frac{1}{2}(a+b)h$ (e) $2l + 2w$ (f) $\pi r l$
    (g) $\dfrac{\pi r^2 h + \pi d l h}{h}$ (h) $\dfrac{\pi r^2 + 2r^2}{r}$

2. In the following expressions, λ is dimensionless and x, y and z have dimensions of length. Explain whether each expression represents a length, area or volume.
    (a) λxy (b) λxyz (c) λy^2
    (d) $\lambda^2 x^2$ (e) $\lambda(x + y + z)$

6.2 3-D Pythagoras

- **You need to be able to apply Pythagoras' theorem in three dimensions.**

Remember:
Pythagoras' theorem:

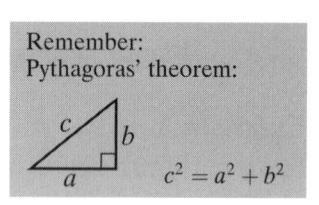

$c^2 = a^2 + b^2$

Example 2

A cuboid measures 3 cm by 5 cm by 10 cm.
Work out the length of the longest diagonal of this cuboid.

First label the vertices A to H as shown.
Then the longest diagonal is AG (or BH, CE or DF).

By Pythagoras: $AG^2 = AC^2 + CG^2$
where $\qquad CG = 10$ cm

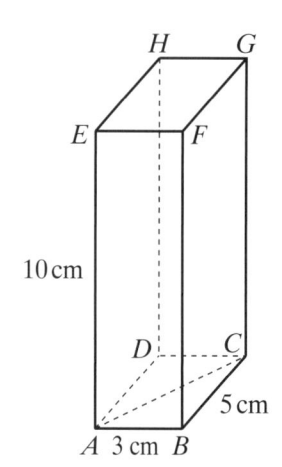

To find AC look at the base $ABCD$:

$$\begin{aligned}\text{Using Pythagoras: } AC^2 &= AB^2 + BC^2 \\ &= 3^2 + 5^2 \\ &= 9 + 25 \\ AC^2 &= 34\end{aligned}$$

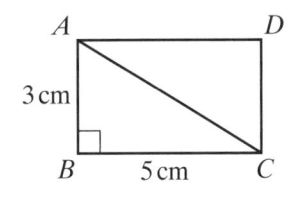

> No need to square root, as you need AC^2.

$$\begin{aligned}\text{Then } AG^2 &= AC^2 + CG^2 \\ &= 34 + 10^2 \\ &= 34 + 100 \\ AG^2 &= 134 \\ \text{So } AG &= \sqrt{134} \\ AG &= 11.58\,\text{cm to 2 d.p.}\end{aligned}$$

> You may be asked to leave the answer in surd form i.e. $\sqrt{134}$ cm.

Exercise 6B

1. Calculate the length of the longest diagonal of a cuboid which has sides 4 cm, 7 cm and 15 cm.

2. Derive an expression for the longest diagonal of a cuboid which measures p cm by q cm by r cm.

3. A cuboid measures 5 cm by 10 cm by 20 cm.
   (a) Calculate the longest possible length across a face.
   (b) Calculate the longest diagonal through the cuboid.

4. A square-based pyramid has base $ABCD$ and vertex V. $AB = 6$ cm and height $= 15$ cm.
   (a) Calculate the length AC.
   (b) Calculate the length AV.

5. A prism $ABCDEF$ has lengths as shown:

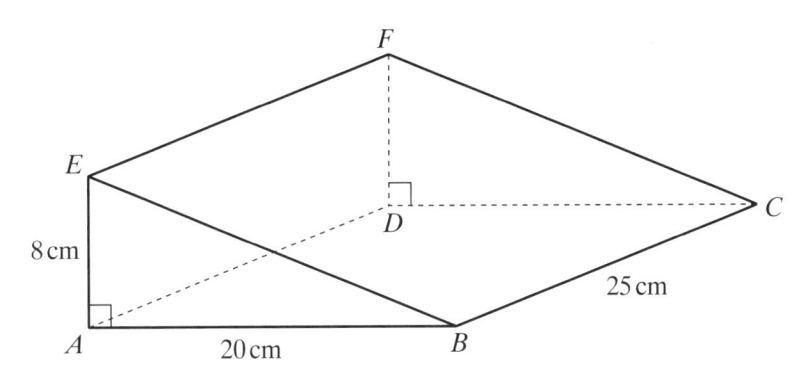

   Calculate:
   (a) EB (b) EC.

6.3 Area of a segment

■ **Area of a segment** = $\dfrac{\pi r^2 \theta}{360} - \tfrac{1}{2} r^2 \sin \theta$

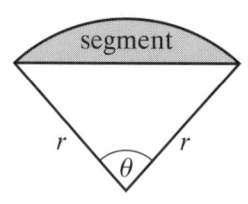

Example 3
Calculate the area of a segment of radius 8 cm and angle 80°.

Area of segment = $\dfrac{\pi r^2 \theta}{360} - \tfrac{1}{2} r^2 \sin \theta$

$= \dfrac{\pi \times 8^2 \times 80}{360} - \tfrac{1}{2} \times 8^2 \times \sin 80°$

$= 44.680 - 31.514$

$= 13.2 \text{ cm}^2$ to 3 s.f.

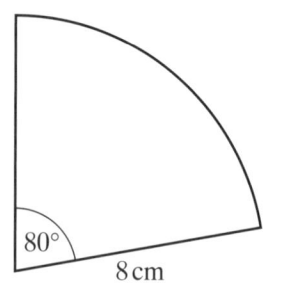

Example 4
The diagram shows a cross-section of a tunnel.

Find the area of the cross-section.

The cross-section is a circle radius 6 m with a segment removed. We will need to find the area of the missing segment.

First find the angle at the centre:

Using $\sin x = \dfrac{\text{opp}}{\text{hyp}}$

$\sin x = \dfrac{5}{6}$

$x = 56.44\ldots°$

So angle of segment = $2 \times x$

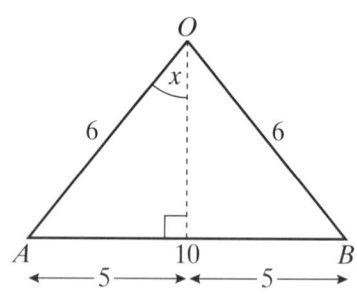

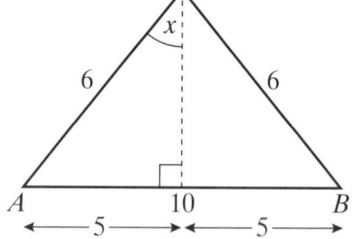

$= 112.89°$

Area of segment = $\dfrac{\pi r^2 \theta}{360} - \tfrac{1}{2} r^2 \sin \theta$

$= \dfrac{\pi \times 6^2 \times 112.89}{360} - \tfrac{1}{2} \times 6^2 \times \sin 112.89$

$= 35.465 - 16.583$

$= 18.882 \text{ cm}^2$

So area of cross-section = $\pi r^2 - 18.882$

$= \pi \times 6^2 - 18.882$

$= 94.2 \text{ m}^2$ to 3 s.f.

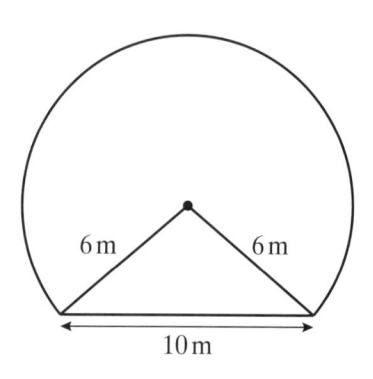

Exercise 6C   Links (*19C*) 19C

1 Calculate the area of each shaded segment, giving your answer:
   (i) to 2 d.p.   **(ii)** in terms of π

(a) 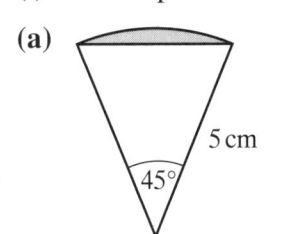 5 cm, 45°

(b) 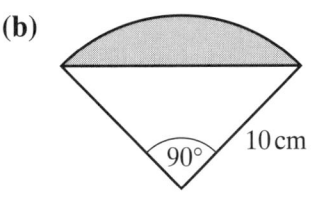 10 cm, 90°

(c) 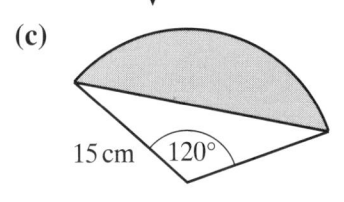 15 cm, 120°

(d) 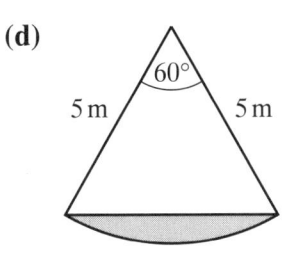 5 m, 5 m, 60°

2 The diagram shows a cross-section of a tunnel. Calculate the area of the cross-section of this tunnel, which is a major segment of a circle radius 4 m.

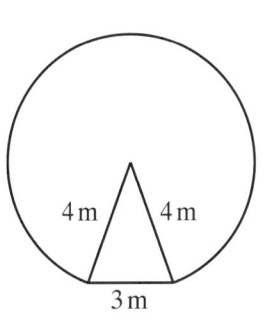

(4 m, 4 m, 3 m)

6.4 Area and volume of similar shapes

- **When a shape is enlarged by scale factor *k* the area of the enlarged shape is k^2 × the area of the original shape.**
- **When a 3-D shape is enlarged by scale factor *k* the volume of the enlarged shape is k^3 × the volume of the original shape.**

Teaching reference:
(pp 349–353, section 19.3)
pp 398–402, section 19.3

Example 5

A good food manufacturer makes two similar boxes, regular and king size. The regular box has a height of 15 cm, and a volume of 1000 cm³. The king size box has a volume of 2500 cm³.
Calculate the height of the king size box.

As they are similar:

$$\text{volume of king size} = k^3 \times \text{volume of regular}$$

$$k^3 = \frac{\text{volume of king size}}{\text{volume of regular}} = \frac{2500}{1000}$$

$$k^3 = 2.5$$

$$k = \sqrt[3]{2.5} = 1.3572 \quad (4 \text{ d.p.})$$

So height of king size = k × height of regular
                       = 1.3572 × 15 = 20.36 cm to 2 d.p.

Advanced measure and mensuration

Exercise 6D Links (*19H*) 19H

1. Lemonade is sold in two sizes of similar bottles, small and giant. The volume of the small bottle is 500 cc, and it has height 10 cm. The volume of the giant bottle is 2 litres. Calculate the height of the giant bottle.

2. Two similar tins of food have heights 5 cm and 12 cm.
   (a) The volume of the smaller tin is 80 cm^3. Calculate the volume of the larger tin.
   (b) The label on the larger tin is 25 cm^2. Calculate the area of the label on the smaller tin.

3. A model aeroplane is built on a scale of 1:50. Copy and complete this table:

Measurement	Aeroplane	Model of aeroplane
Area of roundel	3 m^2	... cm^2
Number of wheels	4	...
Width	... m	6.5 cm
Volume of cabin	... m^3	1600 cm^3

4. The heights of two similar cones are in the ratio 2:5. Calculate the ratio of:
   (a) the surface areas of the cones,
   (b) the volumes of the cones.

5. A model of a factory is built on a scale of 1:60. Calculate the ratio of the volume of the real factory to the volume of the model factory.

6.5 Compound solids

Example 6
Find the volume of this concrete block.
It is made from the bottom part of a cone.

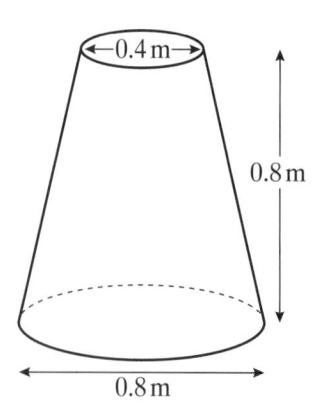

> The proper name for this shape is a 'frustrum'. The frustrum of a cone is the part of the cone cut off between the base and a plane parallel to the base.

The block is part of a cone, height h.

You can find h by similar triangles: $\triangle ABC$ and $\triangle AED$ are similar.

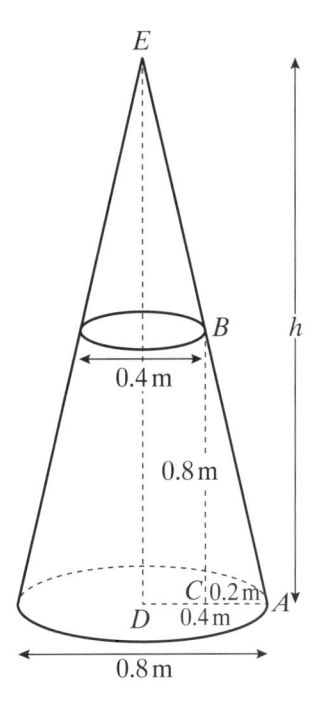

So $\dfrac{h}{0.4} = \dfrac{0.8}{0.2}$

$h = \dfrac{0.4 \times 0.8}{0.2}$

$= 1.6\,\text{m}$

Volume of concrete block

$=$ volume of large cone $-$ volume of small cone

$= \frac{1}{3}\pi \times 0.4^2 \times 1.6 - \frac{1}{3}\pi \times 0.2^2 \times 0.8$

$= \dfrac{0.256\pi}{3} - \dfrac{0.032\pi}{3}$

$= \dfrac{0.224\pi}{3}\,\text{m}^3$

or $0.235\,\text{m}^3$ to 3 s.f.

Remember: volume of a cone
$= \frac{1}{3}\pi r^2 h$

You may be asked to leave your answer in terms of π.

Exercise 6E   Links 19I

1 (a) Find the volume of this frustum. Give your answer (i) correct to 3 s.f. and (ii) in terms of π.

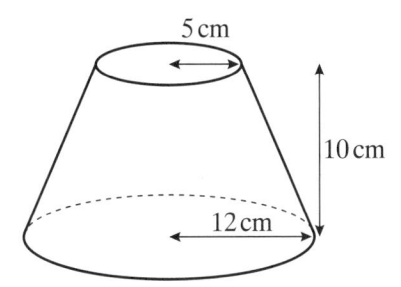

(b) Find the volume of this truncated cone.

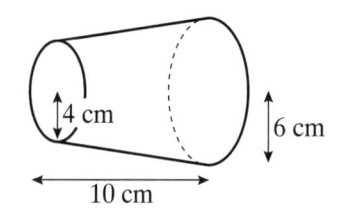

(c) Find the volume of this truncated pyramid.

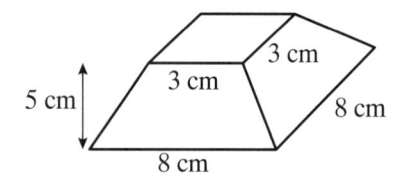

Volume of a pyramid:
$\frac{1}{3}$ × area of base
× vertical height

(d) Find the volume of this frustrum.

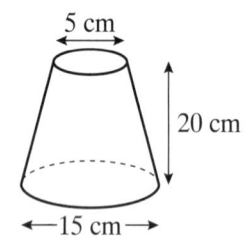

2 This solid is made up from a cone and a hemisphere.
Calculate the volume to 2 d.p.

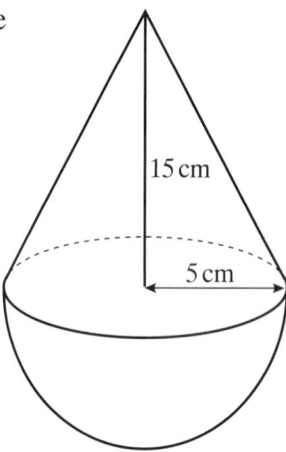

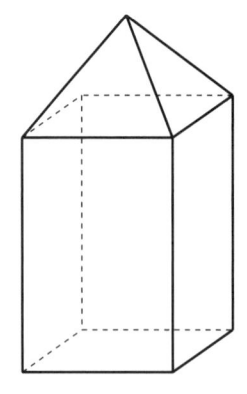

3 Calculate the volume of this church tower.
It is made of a cuboid 5 m × 5 m × 15 m and a square-based pyramid of height 10 m.

4 Calculate the volume of this truncated pyramid correct to 2 d.p.:

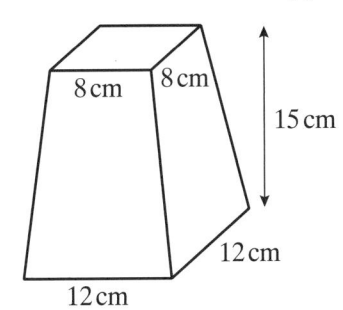

Exercise 6F — Mixed questions

1 Here is the sector of a circle $OABC$ with centre O.
Calculate:
 (a) The arc length ABC
 (b) The chord length AC
 (c) The area of the segment ABC.

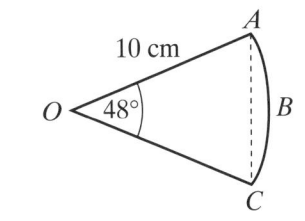

2 In the expression λah^2, λ is dimensionless and a and h have dimensions of length.
Explain whether the expression represents a length, area or volume.

3 The widths of two square-based pyramids are in the ratio $3:7$.
Calculate the ratio of:
 (a) the surface area of the pyramids
 (b) the volume of the pyramids.

4 Calculate the volume of this shape made up of a sphere, a truncated cone and a cylinder. Give your answer in terms of π.

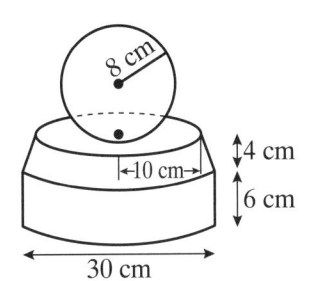

5 $VABC$ is a tetrahedron.
V is the vertex vertically above A. $AV = 12$ cm.
In the base ABC, $B\widehat{A}C = 115°$
Calculate:
 (a) the length BC
 (b) the length VB
 (c) the angle BVC.

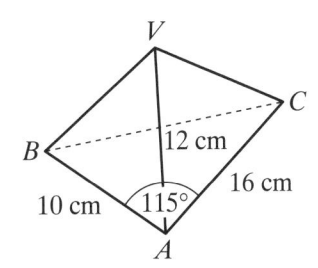

6 VPQRS is a square-based pyramid.
Calculate:
(a) PR
(b) VM (M is the mid-point of PR)
(c) angle VQM
(d) angle PVR.

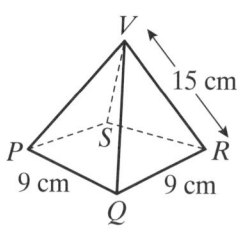

Summary of key points

- $1 \text{ m}^2 = 100 \times 100 \text{ cm}^2 = 10\,000 \text{ cm}^2$

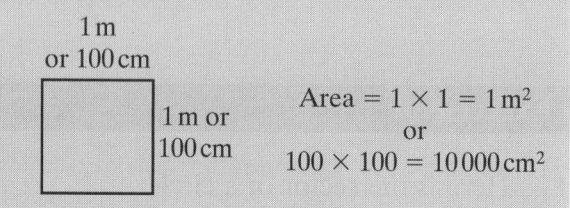

- $1 \text{ m}^3 = 100 \times 100 \times 100 \text{ cm}^3 = 1\,000\,000 \text{ cm}^3$

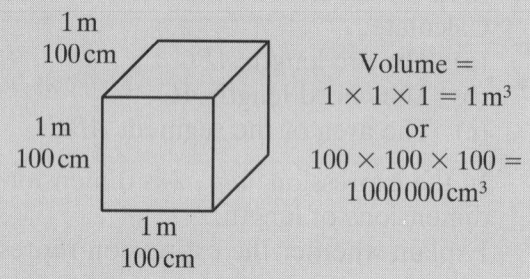

- All formulae for **length** or **distance** have the dimension
    length   and are dimension 1

- All formulae for **area** have the dimensions
    length × length   and are dimension 2

- All formulae for **volume** have the dimensions
    length × length × length   and are dimension 3

- You need to be able to apply Pythagoras' theorem in three dimensions.

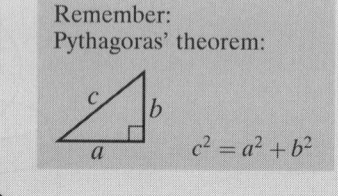

  Remember:
  Pythagoras' theorem:
  $c^2 = a^2 + b^2$

- Area of a segment $= \dfrac{\pi r^2 \theta}{360} - \frac{1}{2} r^2 \sin \theta$

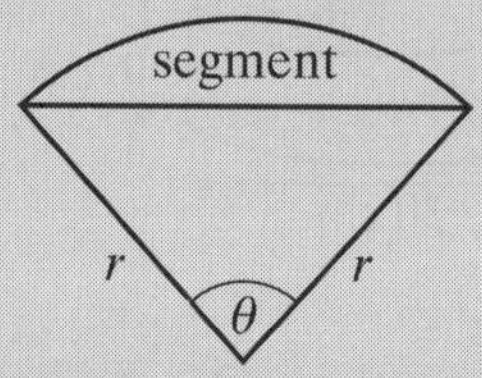

- When a shape is enlarged by scale factor k the area of the enlarged shape is $k^2 \times$ the area of the original shape.

- When a 3-D shape is enlarged by scale factor k the volume of the enlarged shape is $k^3 \times$ the volume of the original shape.

7 Handling data

7.1 Sampling

- **A random sample is one in which each member of the population is equally likely to be selected.**
- **A stratified sample is one in which the population is divided into groups called strata and each stratum is randomly sampled.**
- **A selective sample is one in which every *n*th item is chosen. *n* depends on the size of the sample required.**

> Teaching reference: pp 74–77, section 4.6

> For example, for a 20% sample you would pick every 5th item. You would begin sampling at a randomly chosen number between 1 and 5; if this turned out to be 2, you would pick the 2nd item, the 7th, the 12th, and so on.

Example 1

As part of her statistics project, Sally wishes to take a **random sample** of 30 used cars so that she can record their ages and values. To do this she is going to use the advertisements in *Car Trader* magazine.

The magazine has 200 pages and there are 40 advertisements on each page.

Describe two ways in which Sally could take a **random sample** of size 30.

She could cut out all of the advertisements, screw them up and put them in a bag or box (since the magazine almost certainly has printing on both sides of the paper she will need two copies of the same magazine). The bag or box should then be given a good shake. Sally can then select any 30 of the advertisements from the bag or box.

Alternatively, Sally could number each page in the magazine from 1 to 200, and number each advertisement on each page from 1 to 40. She could then use the RAN# button on her calculator. To do this she must press

   SHIFT   RAN#   to give her a random number between 0 and 1.

She must multiply this random number by 200 – rounding it to an integer to identify the page in the magazine.
Having identified the page, she should again press

   SHIFT   RAN#   to give a second random number between 0 and 1.

She must multiply this second random number by 40 – rounding it to an integer to identify the advertisement on the page.
She should do this whole process 30 times to take her sample. It is possible, though unlikely, that this process will give the same advertisement on more than one occasion. In cases when this happens, Sally should ignore the second result and repeat her process until a different advertisement is selected.

Example 2

A company called Kayman's pack frozen vegetables. They wish to take a selective sample of 5% of a large batch of packets of frozen peas. The peas are packed into the packets directly from a conveyor belt.

Explain how Kayman's could take this selective sample.

5% means 1 in every 20. So firstly they should use a calculator to select a random number between 1 and 20. To do this they could press

SHIFT **RAN#** to give a random number between 0 and 1.

They must then multiply this random number by 20, rounding to the nearest integer. This then identifies the random number between 1 and 20.

Let us assume that the random number was 8. Kayman's should then sample the 8th, 28th, 48th ... packet that passes on the conveyor belt, and so on.

Example 3

James is working on a statistics project in which he is examining the factors which influence the value of used cars.

He has recorded data for three makes of car: **Ford**, **Toyota** and **Mercedes**.

He has also categorized the cars in terms of their sizes of engines as **under 1600 cc** and **1600 cc and over**. The number of cars in each category is recorded in a table as below:

	Ford	Toyota	Mercedes	Total
Under 1600 cc	72	31	18	121
1600 cc and over	41	11	27	79
Total	113	42	45	200

For his project, James wishes to take a stratified sample of 40 cars. This sample must be fairly representative.

How many Mercedes with an engine of 1600 cc or above should James include in his sample?

In his total population, James has 200 cars.
Of these, 27 are Mercedes in the 1600 cc and above category.

As a proportion of the total, this is $\frac{27}{200} = 0.135$.

James's total sample is to be 40. So, to be fairly representative, the number of Mercedes 1600 cc and above included in the sample should be $\frac{27}{200} \times 40 = 5.4$, which rounds down to 5 cars, since it must be a whole number.

> Or simply divide 27 by 5, since 40 is one-fifth of 200; then round down.

Exercise 7A   Links (4D) 4D

1 As part of a statistical project, Kelly needs to interview some students from Jordan Hill County High School. There are 1200 students on the roll of the school.

   (a) Explain how Kelly could select a random sample of 30 students to interview.
   (b) Explain how Kelly could take a selective sample of 4% of the students.

2 Tony is doing a statistical project in which he is looking at the factors which influence the price of second-hand caravans. He has categorized the caravans in terms of the number of berths as:

   2 berth   4 berth   6 berth

He has also categorized them as:

   Mobile   Static

Tony has the following table for the numbers of caravans in each category:

	2 berth	4 berth	6 berth
Mobile	92	166	34
Static	16	26	66
Totals	108	192	100

Tony wishes to take a stratified sample of 50 caravans.

   (a) How many of the caravans in his sample should be static 6 berth caravans if the sample is to be truly representative?
   (b) How many of the caravans in his sample should be 2 berth and mobile if the sample is to be truly representative?

3 (a) Explain the differences between a random sample, a selective sample and a stratified sample.
   (b) Give an example of when it might be best to use
       (i)   a stratified sample
       (ii) a random sample
       (iii) a selective sample.

4 Jennifer is doing a statistics project about the factors which influence the price of a second-hand motorcycle. She is using the advertisements from a magazine called *Bike Trader*. The magazine has 250 pages with 50 advertisements on each page.

Jennifer requires a random sample of 80 advertisements. Describe how she could take such a sample.

5   There are 1400 students at Lassore High School. They are distributed across the year groups and by gender as in the table below:

	Girls	Boys
Year 7	180	170
Year 8	164	160
Year 9	137	142
Year 10	128	118
Year 11	100	101

The governors of the school are considering a possible alteration to the school day. Before any decision is made the Chair of Governors decides to seek the views of the students by interviewing 60 of them.

She wishes to take a stratified sample of 60 students which will be representative across the year groups and the gender divide.

(a) How many boys in Year 10 should the Chair of Governors interview?

(b) Work out the total number of students she should interview who are in Key Stage 3.

6   Explain how a market research company could take a 2% selective sample of people whose names appear in the local telephone directory.

7.2 Grouped data 1

- An estimate can be found for the mean of grouped data by using

$$\bar{x} = \frac{\Sigma fx}{\Sigma f}$$

where x is the mid-point of each class interval.

- Grouped data can be represented using a frequency polygon.
- Information about grouped data can be represented using a cumulative frequency curve.
- The median is the middle value.
- The lower quartile is the value one quarter of the way into the distribution.
- The upper quartile is the value three quarters of the way into the distribution.
- Interquartile range = upper quartile − lower quartile
- The median, lower quartile, upper quartile and range can be represented by using a box plot.

Teaching reference: pp 311–333, sections 15.3, 15.4, 15.5, 15.6, 15.7

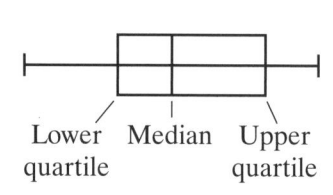

Example 4

A bag contains 80 potatoes.

Information about the distribution of the weights of the potatoes in the bag is given in the table below:

Weight (w) g	Frequency
$0 < w \leqslant 100$	4
$100 < w \leqslant 200$	15
$200 < w \leqslant 300$	36
$300 < w \leqslant 400$	20
$400 < w \leqslant 500$	5

(a) Write down the modal class for this distribution. $200 < W \leqslant 300$
(b) Represent the distribution using a frequency polygon.
(c) Work out an estimate for the mean weight of the potatoes in the bag. $\bar{x} = \frac{\Sigma fx}{\Sigma f}$
(d) Draw the cumulative frequency curve for this distribution.
(e) Use your cumulative frequency curve to find an estimate for:
  (i) the median weight of the potatoes in the bag,
  (ii) the interquartile range of the weights of the potatoes in the bag.
(f) Draw the box plot for this distribution.

(a) The modal class is the class interval with the greatest frequency.

Hence it is the interval $200 < w \leqslant 300$.

(b) The frequency polygon can be drawn like this:

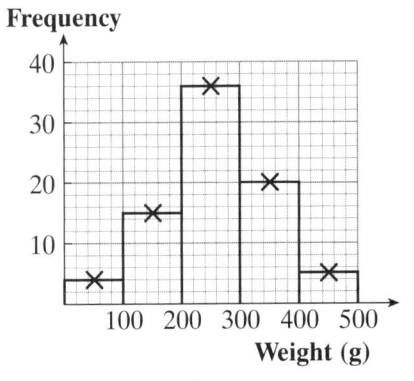

Draw the histogram and mark the mid-points of the bars.

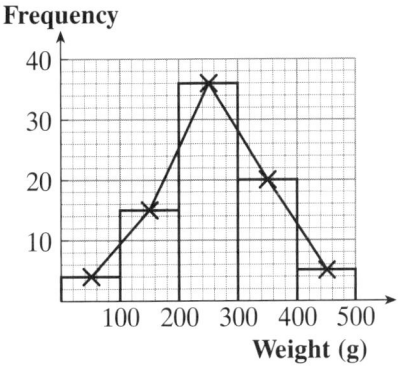

Join the mid-points.

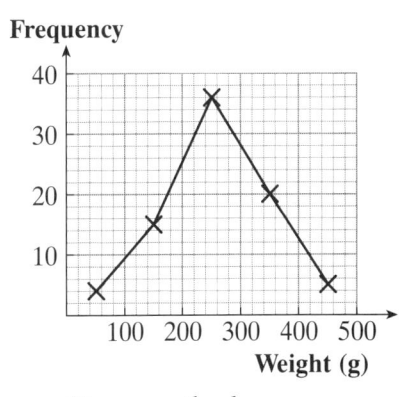

Remove the bars.

(c) The table of mid-points, frequencies and $f \times x$ is as follows:

Mid-point (g)	f	$f \times x$
50	4	200
150	15	2250
250	36	9000
350	20	7000
450	5	2250

Total $= 80 \, (= \Sigma f)$ Total $= 20\,700 \, (= \Sigma fx)$

So the estimated mean is worked out by dividing 20 700 by the number of potatoes in the bag, i.e. the estimated mean weight is

$$\frac{20\,700}{80} = 258.75 \, \text{g}$$

(d) The cumulative frequency table is:

	Cumulative frequency
Up to 100 g	4
Up to 200 g	$4 + 15 = 19$
Up to 300 g	$19 + 36 = 55$
Up to 400 g	$55 + 20 = 75$
Up to 500 g	$75 + 5 = 80$

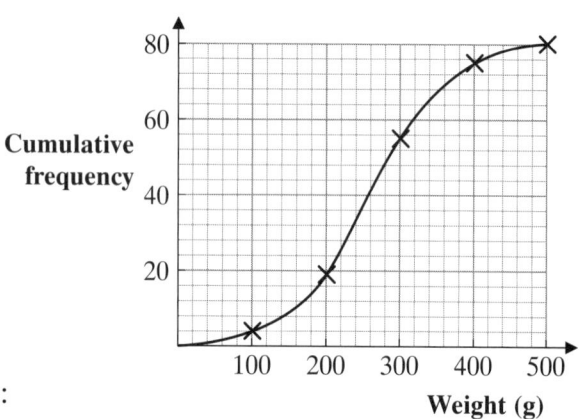

So the cumulative frequency curve is as right:

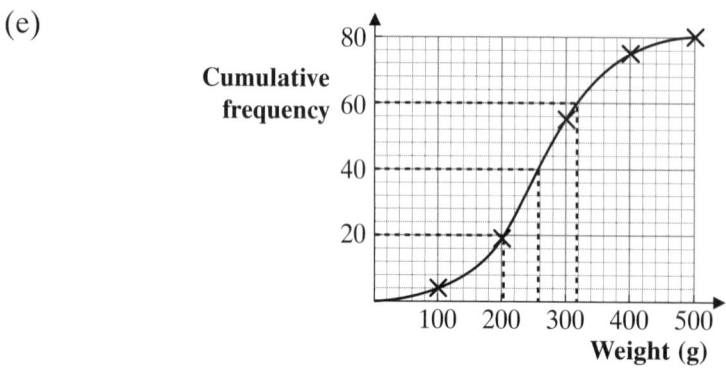

(e)

(i) From the curve, the estimate for the median is 260 g.
(ii) From the curve, the lower quartile and upper quartile can be estimated as 205 g and 320 g respectively.
Thus the estimate for the interquartile range is $320 - 205 = 115$ g

(f) The box plot for the distribution is as shown:

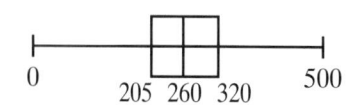

Exercise 7B

1. The police conduct a survey of the speeds of 120 vehicles using a main road. Information about the results of the survey is given in the table right:

Speed (s) mph	Frequency
$0 < s \leq 10$	2
$10 < s \leq 20$	18
$20 < s \leq 30$	24
$30 < s \leq 40$	38
$40 < s \leq 50$	17
$50 < s \leq 60$	10
$60 < s \leq 70$	8
$70 < s \leq 80$	3

   (a) Represent this distribution using a frequency polygon.
   (b) Write down the modal class interval.
   (c) Work out an estimate for the mean speed of these vehicles.
   (d) Draw the cumulative frequency curve for the distribution.
   (e) Use your cumulative frequency curve to find estimates for:
      (i) the median speed of these vehicles,
      (ii) the interquartile range of the speeds,
      (iii) the number of vehicles exceeding a speed of 55 mph.
   (f) Draw a box plot for the distribution.

2. The diagrams below represent three frequency distributions:
   (a)   (b)   (c)

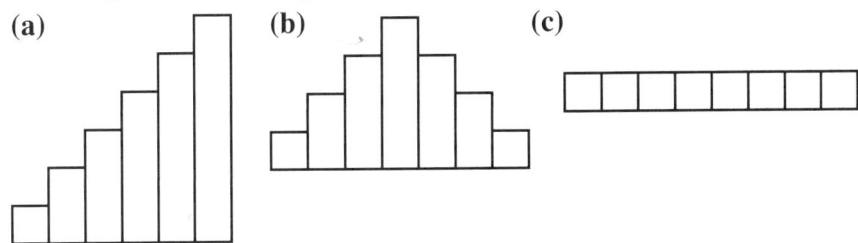

   Sketch the cumulative frequency curve for each distribution.

7.3 Grouped data 2: histograms

Teaching reference: pp 548–560, sections 27.1, 27.2

- A histogram can be drawn for both equal and unequal class intervals.
- When unequal class intervals are used the vertical axis gives frequency density.
- Fundamentally, frequency density = $\dfrac{\text{frequency}}{\text{class width}}$, but the values can be scaled by common factors.
- For any histogram the areas of the rectangles are proportional to the frequencies they represent.

74 Handling data

Example 5

The incomplete table and histogram below provide some information about the ages of the members of Jordan Hill golf club:

Age (a) years	Frequency
0 < a ⩽ 20	20×0·85) =
20 < a ⩽ 30	23
30 < a ⩽ 40	
40 < a ⩽ 50	36
50 < a ⩽ 60	49
60 < a ⩽ 65	
65 < a ⩽ 90	15

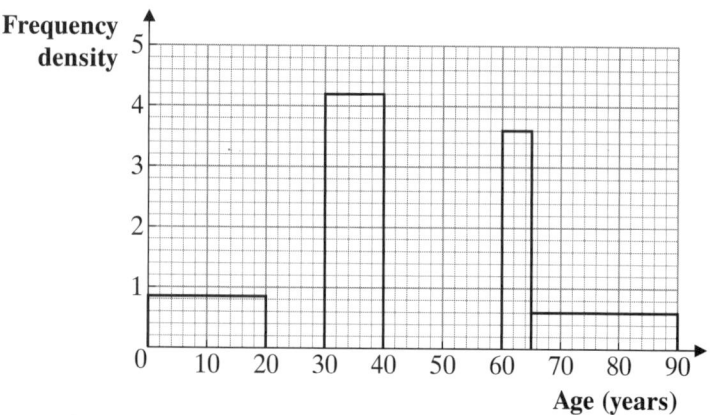

Use the table to complete the histogram, and use the histogram to complete the table.

Using the equation, we can calculate the missing frequency densities for the histogram and use the frequency densities already given to complete the frequency table.

Setting up a table for frequency density:

Age (a) years	Frequency	Frequency density
0 < a ⩽ 20	17 (i.e. 20 × 0.85)	0.85 (from the histogram)
20 < a ⩽ 30	23	2.3 (i.e. 23/10)
30 < a ⩽ 40	42 (4.2 × 10)	4.2
40 < a ⩽ 50	36	3.6 (36/10)
50 < a ⩽ 60	49	4.9 (49/10)
60 < a ⩽ 65	18 (3.6 × 5)	3.6
65 < a ⩽ 90	15	0.6

So the completed table and histogram are as follows:

Age (a) years	Frequency
0 < a ⩽ 20	17
20 < a ⩽ 30	23
30 < a ⩽ 40	42
40 < a ⩽ 50	36
50 < a ⩽ 60	49
60 < a ⩽ 65	18
65 < a ⩽ 90	15

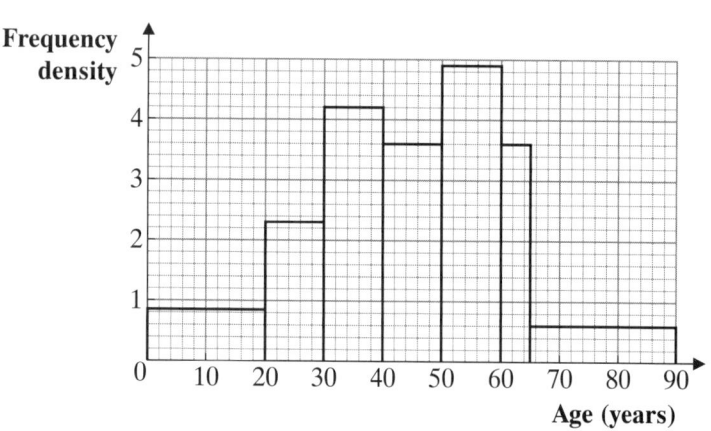

Exercise 7C

1 The incomplete table and histogram below provide information about the distribution of ages of the people living in the village of Shimpwell:

Age (*a*) years	Frequency
$0 < a \leq 15$	20
$15 < a \leq 20$	
$20 < a \leq 30$	42
$30 < a \leq 40$	
$40 < a \leq 65$	57
$65 < a \leq 70$	24
$70 < a \leq 90$	18

(a) Complete the table.
(b) Complete the histogram.
(c) Find the total number of people who live in Shimpwell.
(d) Estimate the number of people living in Shimpwell who are aged between 25 and 40. Give the reasoning behind your answer.

2 Alan is doing a survey of the heights of boys and girls in Year 7. He first takes a random sample of 70 boys from Year 7.

(a) Suggest a suitable method that Alan could use to take a random sample.

The table and the incomplete histogram show information about the boys' heights in this sample of 70 boys.

Heights of boys *h* centimetres	Frequency
$140 \leq h < 145$	10
$145 \leq h < 148$	15
$148 \leq h < 150$	20
$150 \leq h < 154$	16
$154 \leq h < 157$	9

(b) Use the information in the table to complete the histogram.

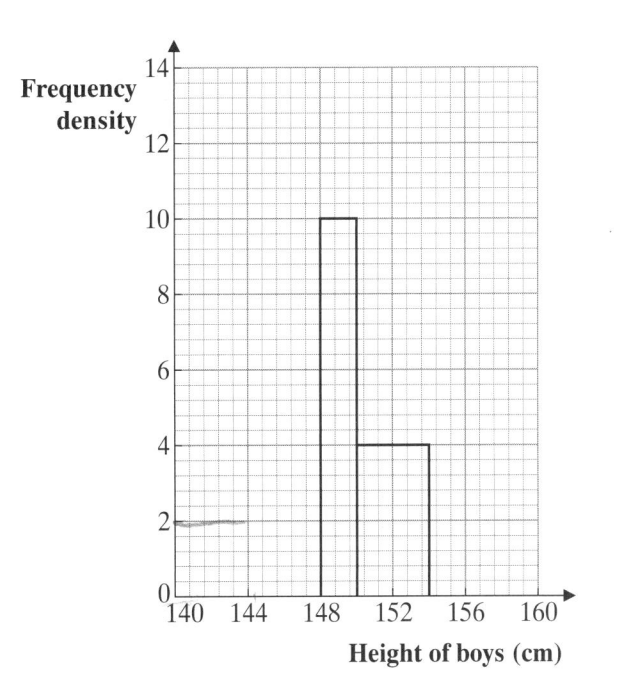

Alan then takes a random sample of 70 girls from Year 7.
The histogram and the incomplete table show information about the girls' heights in this sample of 70 girls.

Heights of girls h centimetres	Frequency
$140 \leq h < 146$	
$146 \leq h < 150$	
$150 \leq h < 151$	
$151 \leq h < 152$	13
$152 \leq h < 155$	21
$155 \leq h < 160$	

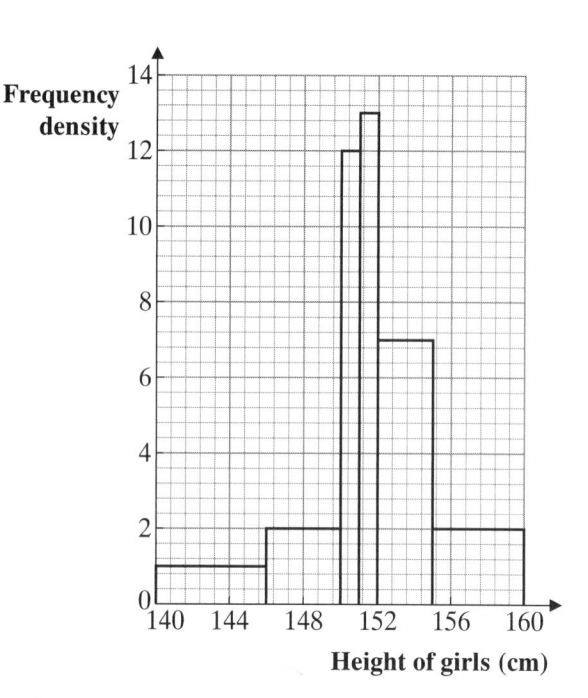

(c) Use the information in the histogram to complete the table.

(d) Use both tables and both histograms to give **two** differences between the distributions of boys' heights and girls' heights. [E]

3 The weights of some babies are given in the table.

Weight W kg	Frequency
$0 \leq W < 2$	0
$2 \leq W < 2.5$	8
$2.5 \leq W < 3$	9
$3 \leq W < 4$	15
$4 \leq W < 6$	27
$W \geq 6$	0

Draw a histogram to show the distribution of weights of the babies.
Use a scale of 2 cm to 1 kg on the weight axis. [E]

7.4 Probability

- **Relative frequency can be used as an estimate for probability.**
- **Relative frequency** = $\dfrac{\text{number of times event occurs}}{\text{total number of trials}}$
- **As the total number of trials increases, so the relative frequency approaches the probability of the event occurring.**
- **When two events, A and B, are mutually exclusive**

    P(A or B) = P(A) + P(B)

Teaching reference: pp 188–199, sections 9.1, 9.2, 9.3, 9.4, 9.5, 9.6

- **For mutually exclusive events**

    P(not A) = 1 − P(A)

- **If two events, A and B, are independent,**

    P(A and B) = P(A) × P(B)

- **Tree diagrams can be used to aid calculations.**

Example 6

The diagram represents a biased spinner:

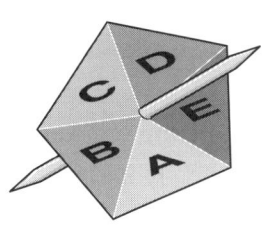

Tom spun the spinner 200 times.
He recorded the section upon which it stopped on each occasion.
His results are given below:

Section	A	B	C	D	E
Frequency	45	27	64	34	30

Asha then spun the same spinner 300 times.
She also recorded the section upon which it landed on each occasion.
Her results are given below:

Section	A	B	C	D	E
Frequency	69	38	98	50	45

(a) Work out the best estimate of the probability of the spinner stopping on section C when it is spun once.

Kenneth spun the spinner 1200 times.
He did not record the face upon which it stopped on any occasion.

(b) Work out the best estimate for the number of times the spinner stopped on face E during the 1200 spins made by Kenneth.

(a) To obtain the best estimate for the probability of the spinner stopping on section C, P(C), we pool Tom's and Asha's results, because the more trials we have, the better our estimate will be.
In $200 + 300 = 500$ spins, the spinner stopped on C on $64 + 98 = 162$ occasions.

$$\text{So our estimate for P(C)} = \frac{\text{number of times spinner stopped on C}}{\text{total number of spins}}$$

$$= \frac{162}{500} = 0.324$$

(b) The best estimate for $P(E) = \dfrac{30 + 45}{500} = \dfrac{75}{500} = 0.15$

But when the spinner is spun 1200 times,

$$P(E) \simeq \dfrac{\text{number of times spinner stops on E}}{1200}$$

So number of times spinner stops on $E = 1200 \times$ best estimate for $P(E)$
$$= 1200 \times 0.15$$
$$= 180$$

Example 7

The probability of a newly laid egg being cracked is 0.008.

(a) Work out the probability of a newly laid egg **not** being cracked.

A supermarket chain orders a batch of 120 000 newly laid eggs.

(b) Work out the best estimate for the number of these eggs which are likely to be cracked.
Give your reasoning.

(a) Probability(not cracked) = 1 − probability(cracked)
$$= 1 - 0.008$$
$$= 0.992$$

(b) Since the batch is a large number, probability(cracked) $= \dfrac{\text{estimated number cracked}}{\text{total in batch}}$

So estimated number cracked = probability(cracked) × total in batch
$$= 0.008 \times 120\,000$$
$$= 960$$

Example 8

The school bus can be either **late** or **not late**.
On any day, the probability of the school bus being **late** = 0.15.

(a) Complete the probability tree diagram for the school bus on Monday and Tuesday.

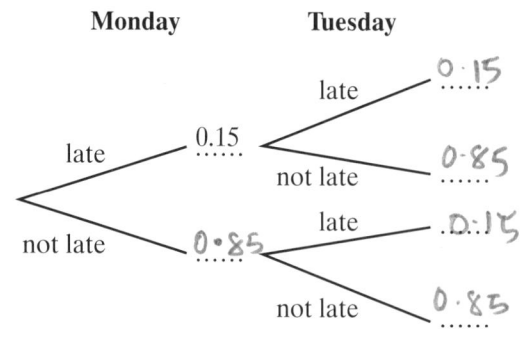

Monday   Tuesday

late — 0.15 — late — 0.15
              not late — 0.85
not late — 0.85 — late — 0.15
                  not late — 0.85

(b) Work out:
   (i) the probability of the school bus being late on both Monday and Tuesday,

$$0.15 \times 0.15 = 0.0225$$

(ii) the probability of the school bus being late on at least one of these two days, 0.85
(iii) the probability of the school bus being late on at least one day during the five days of a school week.

(a) The completed tree diagram is as follows:

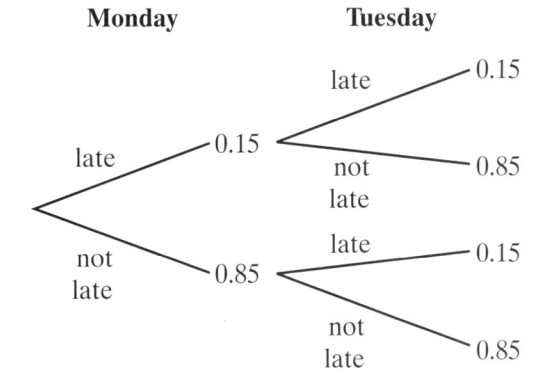

```
            Monday              Tuesday
                                        late    0.15
                      0.15
            late
                                        not     0.85
                                        late
                                        late    0.15
            not       0.85
            late
                                        not     0.85
                                        late
```

(b) (i) The probability of the school bus being late on both days is
$$0.15 \times 0.15 = 0.0225$$

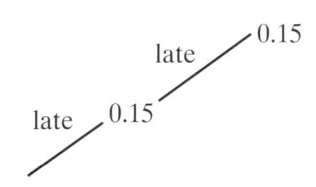

```
                        late    0.15
           late  0.15
```

(ii) To work out the probability of the bus being late on at least one day, we need to consider all of the joint outcomes

late, late or **late, not late** or **not late, late**, not late not late

So the probability is

$0.15 \times 0.15 + 0.15 \times 0.85 + 0.85 \times 0.15$
$= 0.0225 + 0.1275 + 0.1275$
$= 0.2775$

0.15 × 0.15
+ 0.85 × 0.15
+ 0.85 × 0.15
= 0.2775

(iii) The probability of the bus being late on at least one day of the week = 1 − probability of it not being late on all five days.

Probability(not late on all five days) = $0.85^5 = 0.4437$ (to 4 d.p.)

So   0.85⁵

probability of bus being late on at least one day of the week = 1 − 0.4437
$= 0.5563$ (4 d.p.)

Handling data

Exercise 7D

1 When Sarah and Louise play a game of tennis, the probability that Sarah will win is 0.3.
When they play a game of snooker, the probability that Sarah will win is 0.2.
Neither game can ever end in a tie.
Sarah and Louise play a game of tennis and then a game of snooker.
(a) Complete the probability tree diagram:

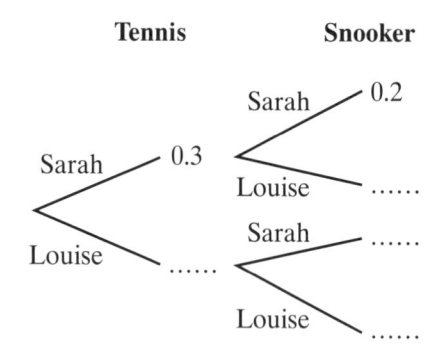

```
        Tennis          Snooker
                     Sarah ─── 0.2
        Sarah ─ 0.3 ─<
       <              Louise ─── ......
        Louise ─ ......
                     Sarah ─── ......
                    <
                     Louise ─── ......
```

(b) Work out the probability of:
  (i) Sarah winning both games,
  (ii) Louise winning at least one of the games.
Next year the girls will play tennis against each other 80 times.
(c) Work out the best estimate for the likely number of these games to be won by Sarah.

2 The probability of a new battery being faulty is 0.03.
(a) Work out the probability of a new battery not being faulty.
A large chain of shops orders 600 000 of these new batteries.
(b) Work out an estimate for the most likely number of these 600 000 batteries that will be faulty.
Aziz buys a pack of three of these batteries.
(c) Work out the probability of all three of these batteries being faulty.
Give your reasoning.

Exercise 7E — Mixed questions

1 The probability of a new computer chip being faulty is 0.0003.
(a) Work out the probability of a new chip not being faulty.
A company produces 12 million of these chips.
(b) Work out an estimate of the most likely number of these chips to be faulty.

2 Mrs Parvesi, the deputy head teacher at Jordan Hill High School, wishes to select a random sample of 50 girls at the school. Explain how she could do this.

3   The table below provides information about the speeds of 120 vehicles on a road:

Speed (s) mph	Frequency
$20 < s \leqslant 30$	14
$30 < s \leqslant 40$	22
$40 < s \leqslant 50$	36
$50 < s \leqslant 60$	25
$60 < s \leqslant 70$	16
$70 < s \leqslant 80$	7

(a) Give an estimate of the mean speed.
(b) Draw the frequency polygon.
(c) Complete a cumulative frequency table.
(d) Draw the cumulative frequency curve.
(e) Find an estimate of the median speed.
(f) Find estimates for:
   (i)   the lower quartile speed
   (ii) the upper quartile speed
   (iii) the interquartile range of speeds.
(g) Draw the box plot for this distribution.

4   The incomplete table and histogram provide some information about the speeds of vehicles on a motorway. Complete the table and histogram.

Speed (s) mph	Frequency
$0 < s \leqslant 30$	
$30 < s \leqslant 40$	40
$40 < s \leqslant 50$	
$50 < s \leqslant 60$	30
$60 < s \leqslant 80$	
$80 < s \leqslant 100$	10

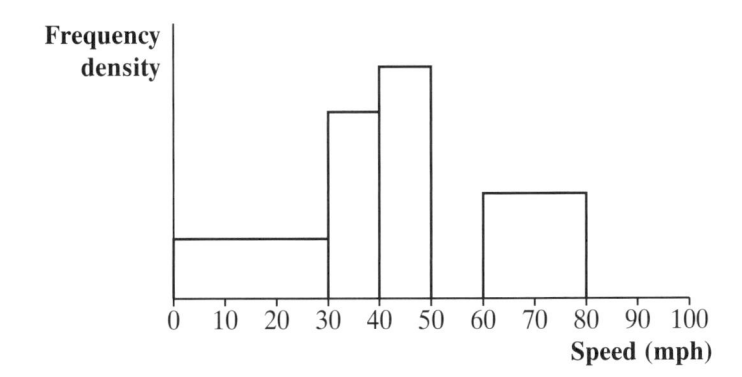

5 When Jim and Andy play a game of snooker, the probability of Jim winning is 0.8.
When they play a game of tennis, the probability of Jim winning is 0.3.
Tomorrow they are due to play a game of snooker and a game of tennis.
(a) Work out the probability of Jim losing both games.
(b) Work out the probability of Andy winning at least one game.

6 Sketch the histogram for the following cumulative frequency curve, using equal class intervals.

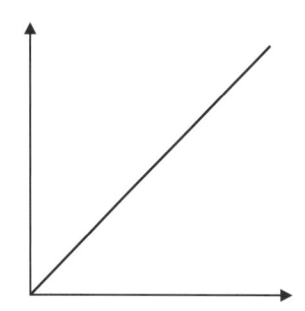

Summary of key points

- A random sample is one in which each member of the population is equally likely to be selected.
- A stratified sample is one in which the population is divided into groups called strata and each stratum is randomly sampled.
- A selective sample is one in which every nth item is chosen. n depends on the size of the sample required.
- An estimate can be found for the mean of grouped data by using

$$\bar{x} = \frac{\Sigma fx}{\Sigma f}$$

  where x is the mid-point of each class interval.
- Grouped data can be represented using a frequency polygon.
- Information about grouped data can be represented using a cumulative frequency curve.
- The median is the middle value.
- The lower quartile is the value one quarter of the way into the distribution.
- The upper quartile is the value three quarters of the way into the distribution.

- Interquartile range = upper quartile − lower quartile
- The median, lower quartile, upper quartile and range can be represented by using a box plot.
- A histogram can be drawn for both equal and unequal class intervals.
- When unequal class intervals are used the vertical axis gives frequency density.
- Fundamentally, frequency density = $\dfrac{\text{frequency}}{\text{class width}}$, but the values can be scaled by common factors.
- For any histogram the areas of the rectangles are proportional to the frequencies they represent.
- Relative frequency can be used as an estimate for probability.
- Relative frequency = $\dfrac{\text{number of times event occurs}}{\text{total number of trials}}$
- As the total number of trials increases, so the relative frequency approaches the probability of the event occurring.
- When two events, A and B, are mutually exclusive

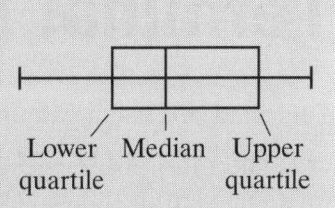

    P(A or B) = P(A) + P(B)

- For mutually exclusive events

    P(not A) = 1 − P(A)

- If two events, A and B, are independent,

    P(A and B) = P(A) × P(B)

- Tree diagrams can be used to aid calculations.

Terminal practice paper 1

You must not use a calculator.

1. The ratio of the ages of two women is 5:4.
   The sum of their ages is 63 years.
   Find their ages. (2)

2. (a) Simplify: (i) $(x^7)^3$ (ii) $(5y^4)^2$ (2)

   (b) Simplify $\dfrac{30(t-2)^2}{5(t-2)}$. (2)

3.

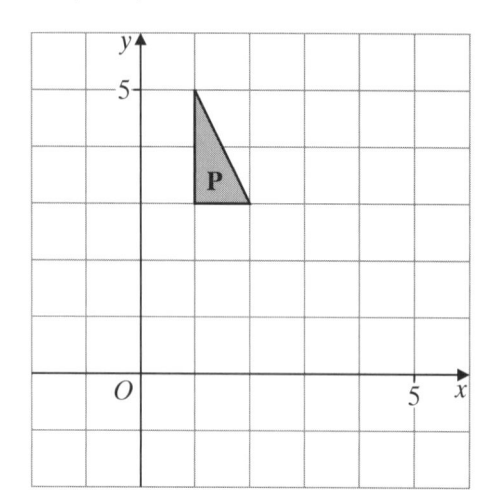

   (a) Translate triangle **P** by the vector $\begin{pmatrix} 2 \\ -2 \end{pmatrix}$.
   Label the new triangle **Q**. (2)
   (b) Reflect triangle **Q** in the line with equation $y = x$.
   Label the new triangle **R**. (2)
   (c) Describe fully the single transformation which maps triangle **P** onto triangle **R**. (2)

4. (a) Work out an estimate for the value of $\sqrt{\dfrac{476 \times 18.9}{234}}$. (3)

   (b) Make E the subject of the formula $v = \sqrt{\dfrac{2E}{m}}$. (2)

5. Tom has two bags of letter tiles.
   Tiles with the letters A, B and C are in one bag and tiles with the letters D, E, F and G are in the other bag.
   He picks a tile at random from each bag.
   (a) Show the combined outcomes in a tree diagram. (2)
   (b) List the combined outcomes. (1)

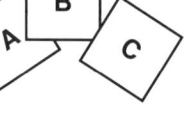

Tom repeats the experiment with 7 tiles in one bag and 5 tiles in the other bag. The tiles all have different letters.
(c) Work out the number of combined outcomes. (1)
'Tom's choice of tile from one bag is independent of his choice of tile from the other bag.'
(d) Explain the meaning of this statement. (1)

6 The diameter of a semicircle is 6 cm.
Find, in terms of π,
(a) the area of the semicircle,
(b) the total perimeter of the semicircle. (5)

7 Evaluate: (a) $16^{\frac{1}{4}}$ (b) $25^{\frac{3}{2}}$ (c) $8^{-\frac{2}{3}}$ (3)

8 y is directly proportional to x^2.
$y = 20$ when $x = 2$.
(a) Express y in terms of x. (3)
(b) Find the value of y when $x = 3$. (1)

9 (a) Rationalize $\dfrac{20}{\sqrt{5}}$. (2)

(b) Expand $(\sqrt{5} - 2)^2$.
Give your answer in the form $a + b\sqrt{5}$. (2)

10

Diagram NOT accurately drawn.

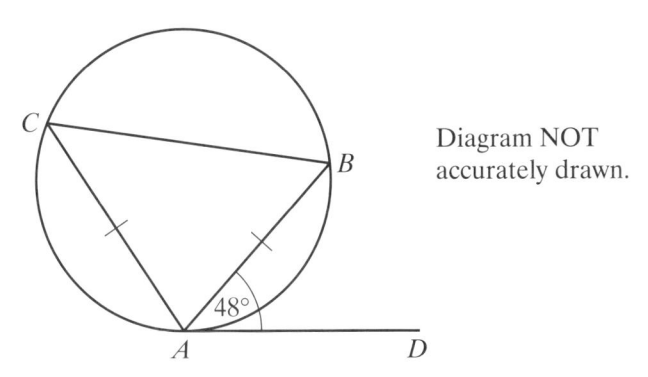

A, B and C are points on the circumference of a circle.
A tangent is drawn from D to touch the circle at A.
Angle $BAD = 48°$.
$AB = AC$.
Calculate the size of angle ABC.
Give reasons for your answer. (4)

11 Solve the equation $x^2 - x - 6 = 0$ by drawing the graph of $y = x^2 + 2x - 3$ for $-3 \leqslant x \leqslant 4$ and an appropriate straight line. (4)

12 The histogram shows information about the examination marks of some candidates:

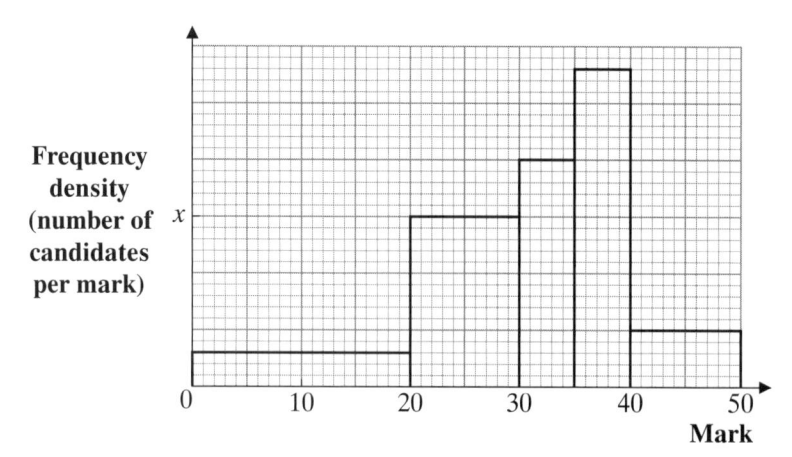

150 candidates scored a mark greater than or equal to 20 and less than 30.

(a) Find the value of x. (1)

The pass mark for the examination was 31.

(b) 'Exactly half the candidates passed.'
Do you agree or disagree with this statement?
Justify your answer. (5)

13 Solve the simultaneous equations $2x + y = 3$
$x^2 + y^2 = 18$ (7)

14 (a) Sketch the graph of $y = 3 \sin 10t$ for $0 \leqslant t \leqslant 36$. (3)
(b) Use your sketch to explain why $3 \sin 10t = 1$ has two solutions in the range $0 \leqslant t \leqslant 36$. (1)

Terminal practice paper 2

You may use a calculator.

1. (a) Find the value of $\sqrt{\dfrac{8.1^2}{2.6^3}}$.

    Write down all the figures on your calculator display. (1)
   (b) Give your answer to part (a) correct to 3 significant figures. (1)

2.

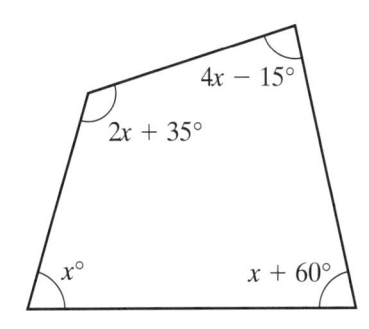

    Work out the value of x. (4)

    (Angles shown: $x°$, $2x + 35°$, $4x - 15°$, $x + 60°$)

3. The density of tin is 7310 kg/m^3.
   Calculate the weight, in **grams**, of 63 cm^3 of tin. (4)

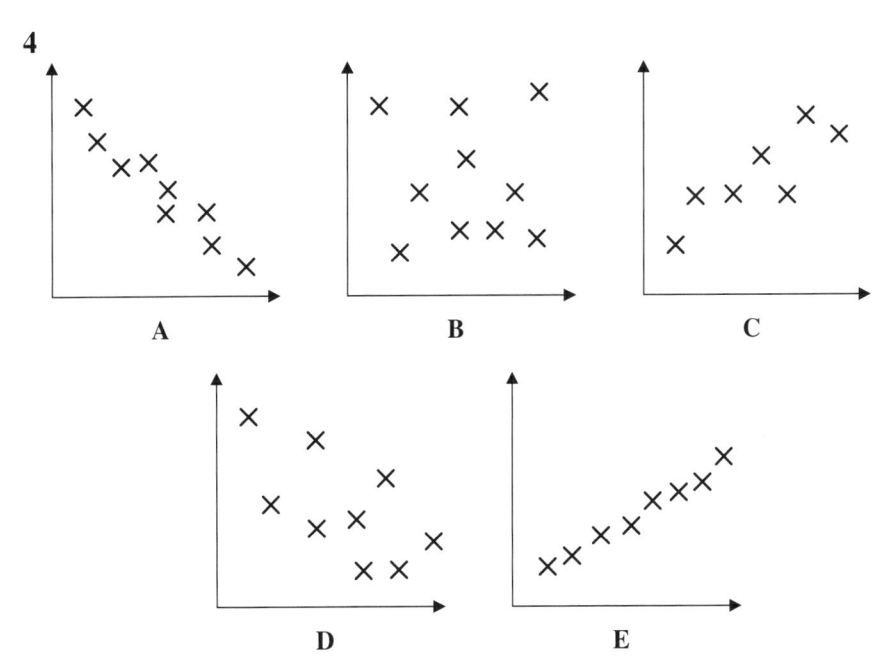

4. Write down the letter of the scatter graph which shows:
   (i) high positive correlation, (ii) low positive correlation,
   (iii) no correlation, (iv) high negative correlation,
   (v) low negative correlation. (5)

5 In a sale, all the normal prices are reduced by 15%.
The sale price of a television is £539.75.
Calculate the normal price of the television. (3)

6 Draw a diagram to show the region which satisfies all three of the inequalities $y \leqslant 6$, $y \geqslant x$ and $x + y > 6$. (4)

7

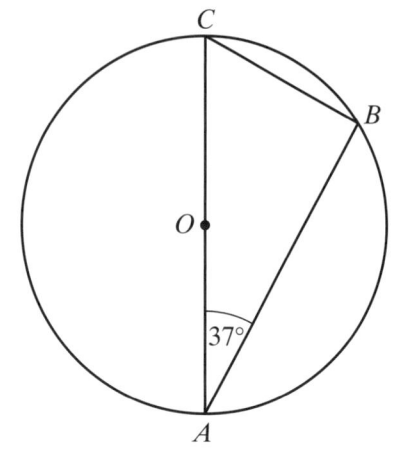

Diagram NOT accurately drawn.

A, B and C are points on the circumference of a circle, centre O.
AC is a diameter of the circle.
Angle $BAC = 37°$.
Find the size of angle ACB. (2)

8 A line **L** passes through the point with coordinates (4, 1) and is parallel to the line with equation $y = 2x + 3$.
(a) Find the equation of the line **L**. (2)
A line **M** passes through the point with coordinates (4, 1) and is perpendicular to the line with equation $y = 2x + 3$.
(b) Find the equation of the line **M**. (2)

9 A runner covers 100 m in 11.6 seconds.
The distance is accurate to the nearest metre and the time is accurate to the nearest 0.1 second.
(a) Calculate the upper bound for the runner's average speed in m/s. (3)
(b) Write the runner's average speed to an appropriate degree of accuracy.
Explain your answer. (3)

10 (a) Factorize $3x^2 - 75$. (2)

(b) Simplify fully $\dfrac{3x^2 - 75}{4x^2 - 17x - 15}$. (3)

11

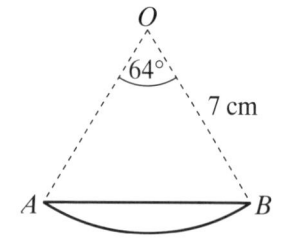

Diagram NOT accurately drawn.

The diagram shows a segment of a circle with centre O and radius 7 cm.
AB is a chord of the circle.
AB subtends an angle of 64° at O.
Calculate the area of the segment.
Give your answer correct to 3 significant figures. (5)

12 The table shows information about the age distribution of male students at Mathstown College:

Age (years)	Number of male students
16	97
17	224
18	179

Kate carried out a survey about the students' part-time jobs.
She used a stratified sample of 60 male students according to age.
(a) Calculate the number of students of each age which should have been in her sample of 60. (3)
Kate also used a stratified sample of 60 female students according to age.
In the college, there were 193 female students aged 17 years.
In Kate's sample, there were 22 female students aged 17 years.
(b) Calculate the smallest possible number of female students there could be in the college. (3)

13

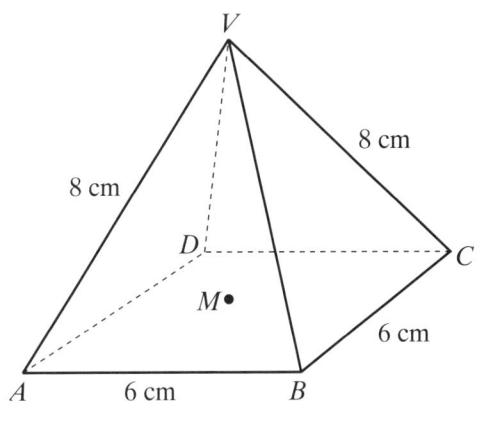

Diagram NOT accurately drawn.

The diagram shows a square-based pyramid $ABCDV$.
M is the mid-point of the square base $ABCD$.
The vertex V is vertically above M.
The length of each side of the square base is 6 cm.
The length of each sloping edge is 8 cm.
(a) Calculate the length of MV.
Give your answer correct to 3 significant figures. (3)
(b) Calculate the size of the angle AV makes with the base.
Give your answer correct to one decimal place. (3)

14 (a) Express $x^2 - 4x$ in the form $(x+p)^2 + q$, where p and q are integers. (2)

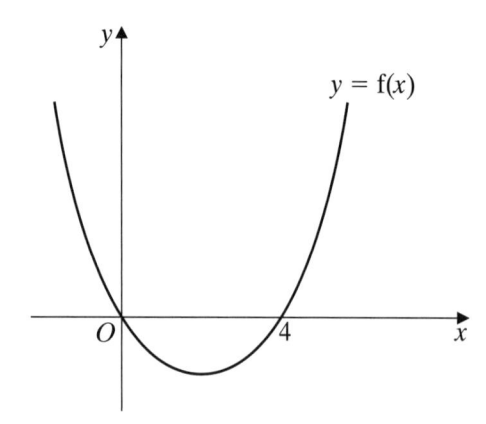

The diagram shows a sketch of part of the curve $y = \text{f}(x)$, where $\text{f}(x) = x^2 - 4x$.
(b) Sketch the graph of:
    (i) $y = \text{f}(x) + 2$ (ii) $y = 2\text{f}(x)$ (4)

Answers

Exercise 1A

1 (a) $(-1, 1)$ and $(2, 4)$

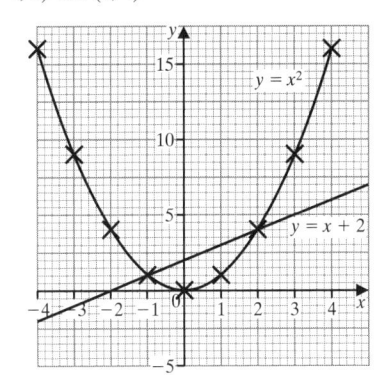

(b) $(1, 1)$ and $(3, 9)$

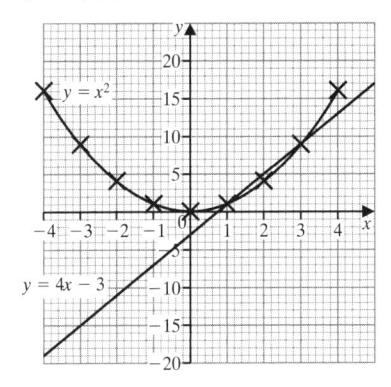

(c) $(-1, 5)$ and $(-3, 13)$

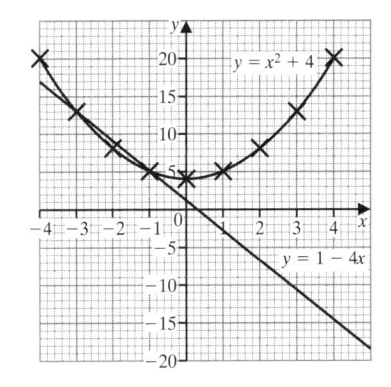

(d) $(-2, -2)$ and $(1, 1)$

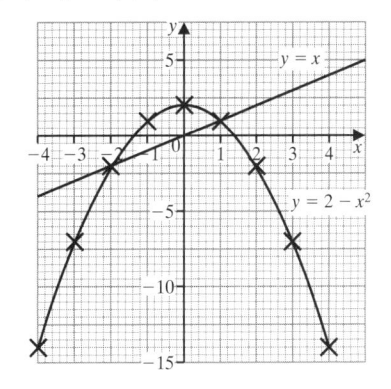

(e) $(-3, 11)$ and $(2, 6)$

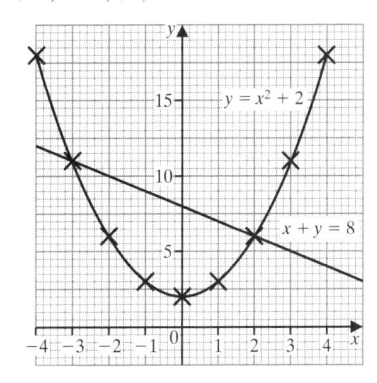

(f) $(-1, 8)$ and $(3, 0)$

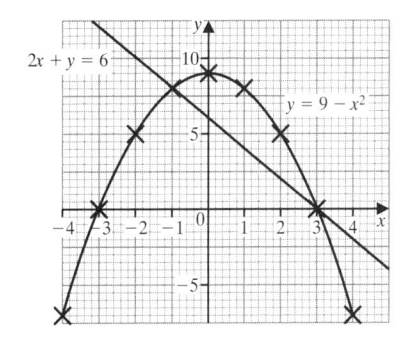

92 Answers

(g) $(-2, -3)$ and $(-1, -2)$

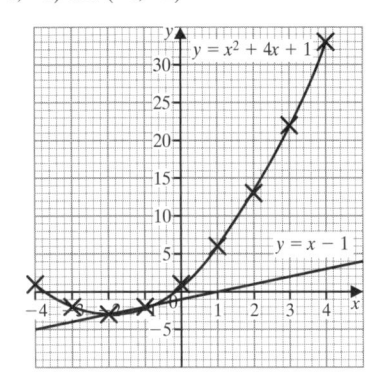

(h) $(-1, 4)$ and $(2, 1)$

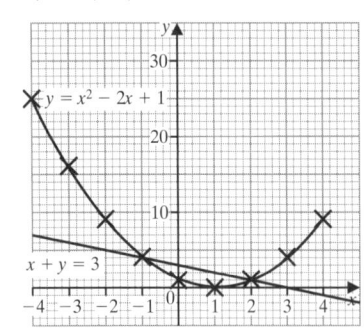

2 (a) $x = -2, y = 4$ and $x = 3, y = 9$

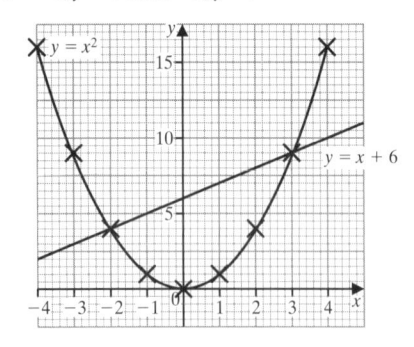

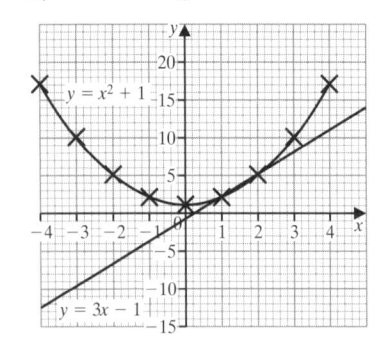

(b) $x = 1, y = 2$ and $x = 2, y = 5$

(c) $x = -3, y = 7$ and $x = 1, y = -1$

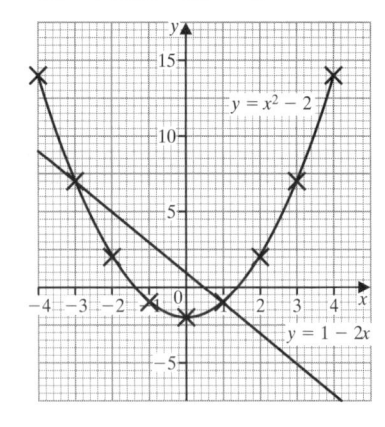

(d) $x = -3, y = -5$ and $x = -1, y = 3$

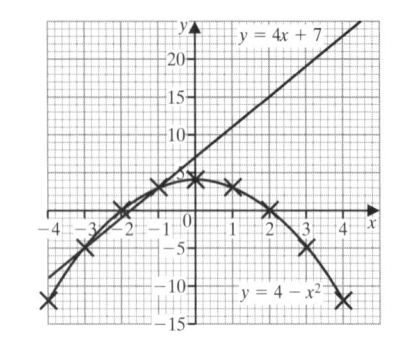

(e) $x = -1, y = 2$ and $x = 2, y = -1$

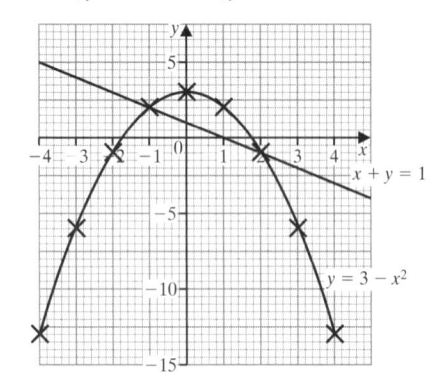

(f) $x = -2, y = 12$ and $x = -1, y = 9$

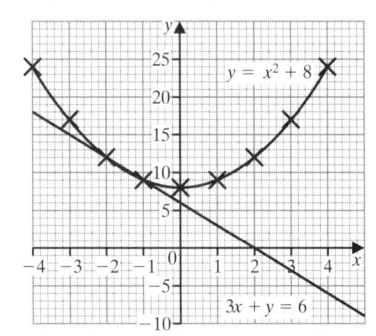

(g) $x = 1, y = -1$ and $x = 3, y = 3$

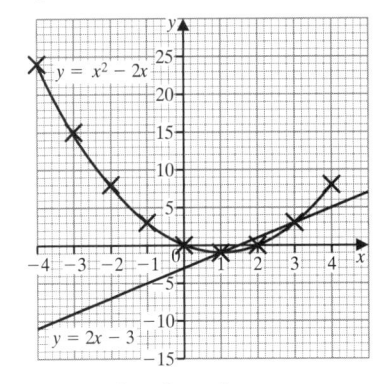

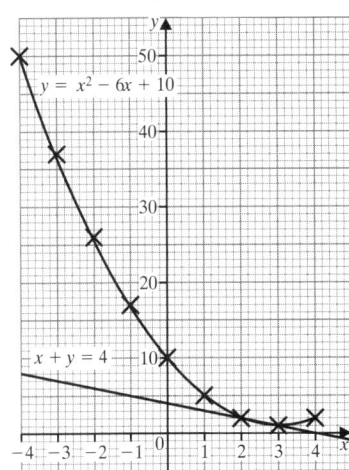

(h) $x = 2, y = 2$ and $x = 3, y = 1$

3 (a) (b)

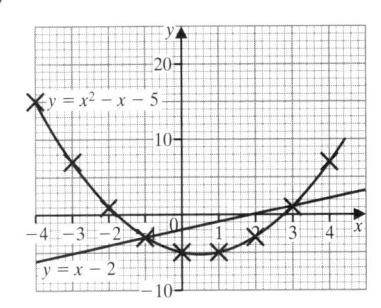

(b) $x = 3, x = -1$

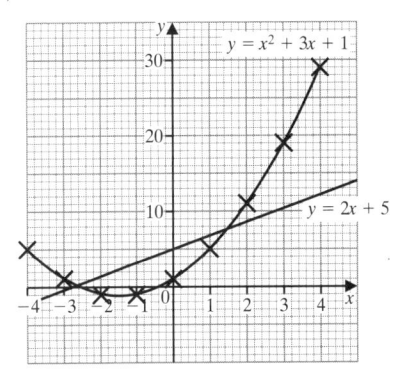

4 (a) (b)

(b) $x = 1.6, x = -2.6$ (1 d.p.)

5 (a) (1, 3)

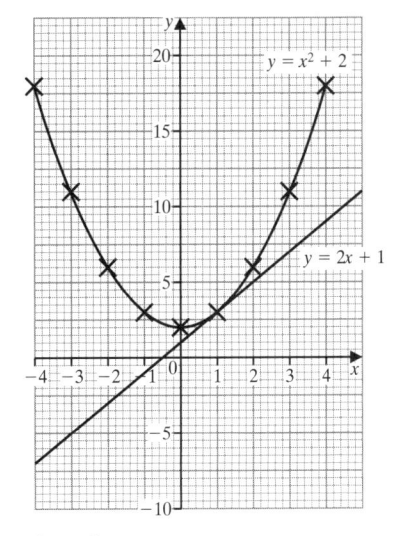

(b) $x = 1, y = 3$

Exercise 1B

1 (a) $x = 1, y = 1$ and $x = 4, y = 16$
   (b) $x = -1, y = 1$ and $x = 5, y = 25$
   (c) $x = -4, y = 17$ and $x = 2, y = 5$
   (d) $x = -5, y = 17$ and $x = 4, y = 8$
   (e) $x = -5, y = -16$ and $x = 2, y = 5$
   (f) $x = -6, y = 33$ and $x = 3, y = 6$
   (g) $x = -7, y = -10$ and $x = -1, y = -4$
   (h) $x = -7, y = 31$ and $x = 2, y = 4$
2 (a) $x = \frac{1}{2}, y = \frac{1}{2}$ and $x = 3, y = 18$
   (b) $x = -1, y = 3$ and $x = \frac{2}{3}, y = 1\frac{1}{3}$
   (c) $x = -\frac{3}{5}, y = 3\frac{4}{5}$ and $x = 1, y = 7$
   (d) $x = -2, y = 1$ and $x = 2\frac{1}{2}, y = 5\frac{1}{2}$
   (e) $x = -1\frac{1}{2}, y = -3$ and $x = \frac{1}{2}, y = 5$
   (f) $x = -\frac{3}{4}, y = 13\frac{3}{4}$ and $x = \frac{1}{3}, y = 8\frac{1}{3}$
   (g) $x = -\frac{1}{2}, y = 2$ and $x = 1\frac{1}{3}, y = 5\frac{2}{3}$
   (h) $x = -1\frac{1}{2}, y = 8$ and $x = 1\frac{1}{5}, y = 2\frac{3}{5}$
3 (a) (2, 10) and (5, 31)
   (b) (−9, −77) and (1, 3)
   (c) (−1, 2) and $(2\frac{1}{2}, 12\frac{1}{2})$
   (d) $(\frac{3}{5}, 3\frac{4}{5})$ and (3, 47)
   (e) $(\frac{1}{3}, 1)$ and (4, 23)
   (f) $(-\frac{2}{3}, 3\frac{2}{3})$ and $(-\frac{1}{2}, 3\frac{1}{2})$
   (g) $(-1\frac{2}{3}, 36\frac{2}{3})$ and $(\frac{3}{4}, 12\frac{1}{2})$
4 (3, 17)
5 (a) $x = \frac{1}{2}, y = 8\frac{1}{2}$
   (b) The parabola $y = 9 - 2x^2$ and the line $4x + 2y = 19$ intersect at only one point, $(\frac{1}{2}, 8\frac{1}{2})$, so the line is a tangent to the parabola.

Answers

Exercise 1C

1. (a) $(-4, -3)$ and $(3, 4)$

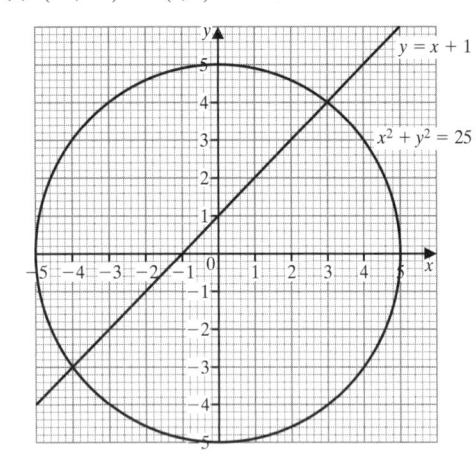

(b) $(0, -10)$ and $(6, 8)$

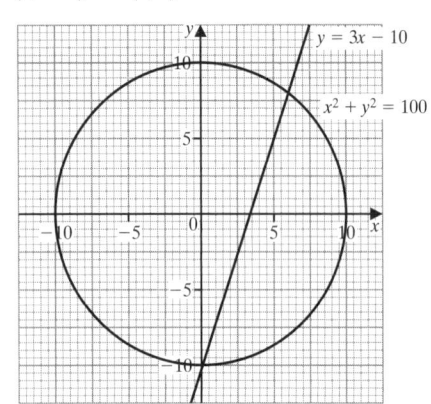

(c) $(-3, 4)$ and $(4, -3)$

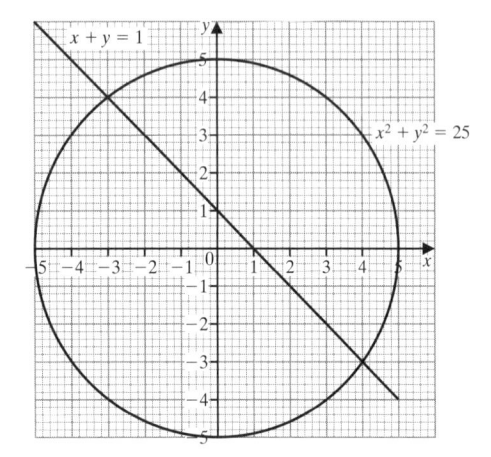

(d) $(0, 10)$ and $(8, 6)$

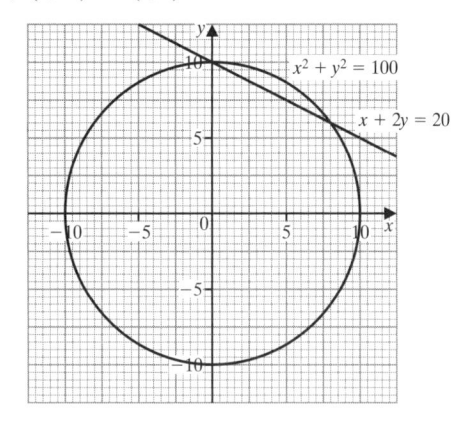

(e) $(0, 3)$ and $(3, 0)$

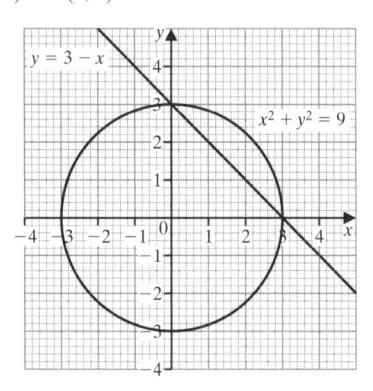

2. (a) $x = -6, y = -8$ and $x = 8, y = 6$

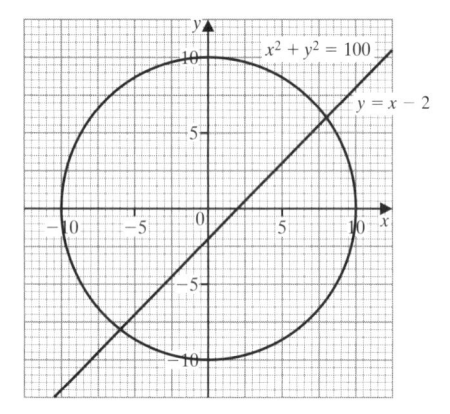

(b) $x = -3, y = -4$ and $x = 0, y = 5$

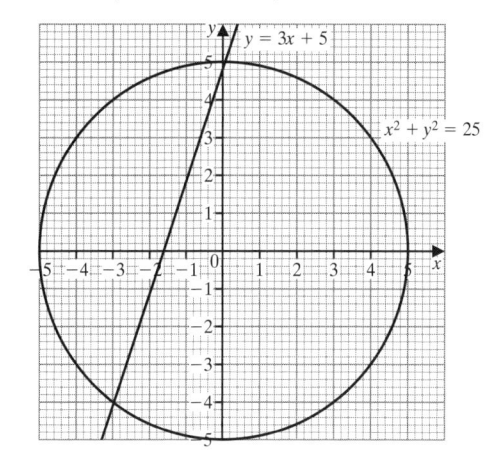

(c) $x = -4, y = 3$ and $x = 3, y = -4$

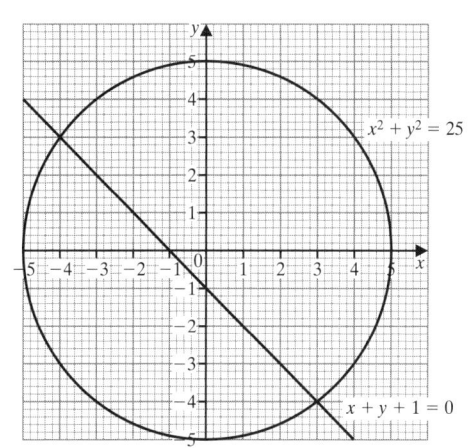

(d) $x = -8, y = 6$ and $x = 0, y = 10$

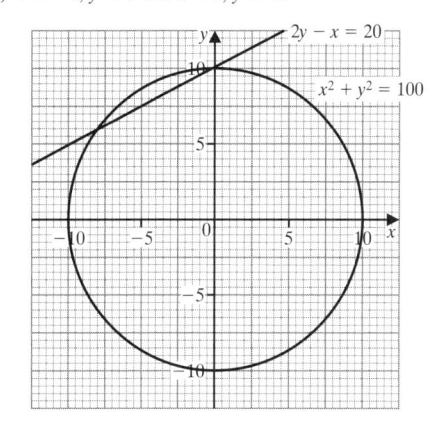

(e) $x = 0, y = 4$ and $x = 4, y = 0$

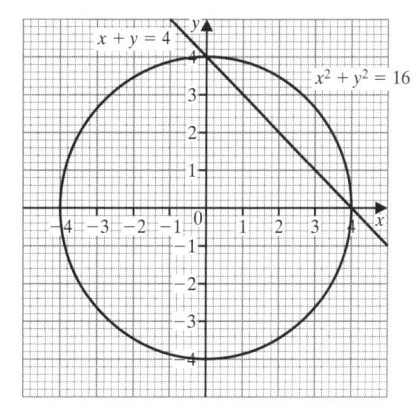

3 (a) $(6, -8)$

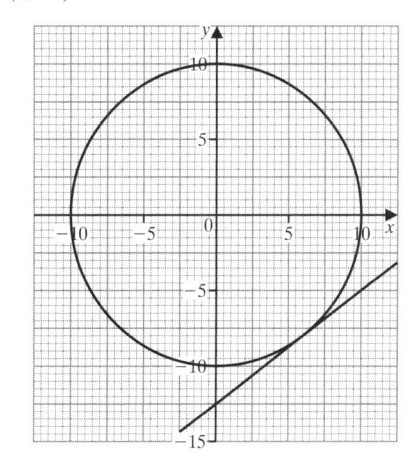

(b) $x = 6, y = -8$

Exercise 1D

1 (a) $x = -3, y = -2$ and $x = 2, y = 3$
  (b) $x = -3, y = -5$ and $x = 5, y = 3$
  (c) $x = -3, y = 6$ and $x = 6, y = -3$
  (d) $x = 0, y = -7$ and $x = 7, y = 0$
  (e) $x = \frac{2}{5}, y = -2\frac{1}{5}$ and $x = 2, y = 1$
  (f) $x = -1, y = -1$ and $x = 1\frac{2}{5}, y = \frac{1}{5}$

2 (a) $x = -6, y = 2$ and $x = 6, y = 2$. The line $y = 2$ intersects the circle $x^2 + y^2 = 40$ at two points, $(-6, 2)$ and $(6, 2)$.
  (b) $x = -7, y = -1$ and $x = 1, y = 7$. The line $y = x + 6$ intersects the circle $x^2 + y^2 = 50$ at two points, $(-7, -1)$ and $(1, 7)$.
  (c) $x = 1, y = -4$ and $x = 4, y = -1$. The line $y = x - 5$ intersects the circle $x^2 + y^2 = 17$ at two points, $(1, -4)$ and $(4, -1)$.
  (d) $x = -2, y = 2$. The line $y = x + 4$ intersects the circle $x^2 + y^2 = 8$ at one point, $(-2, 2)$. The line is a tangent to the circle.
  (e) $x = -2, y = -5$ and $x = 1\frac{2}{5}, y = 5\frac{1}{5}$. The line $y = 3x + 1$ intersects the circle $x^2 + y^2 = 29$ at two points, $(-2, -5)$ and $(1\frac{2}{5}, 5\frac{1}{5})$.
  (f) $x = 3, y = 3$. The line $x + y = 6$ intersects the circle $x^2 + y^2 = 18$ at one point, $(3, 3)$. The line is a tangent to the circle.
  (g) $x = -\frac{4}{5}, y = 4\frac{2}{5}$ and $x = 2, y = -4$. The line $3x + y = 2$ intersects the circle $x^2 + y^2 = 20$ at two points, $(-\frac{4}{5}, 4\frac{2}{5})$ and $(2, -4)$.

96 Answers

(h) $x = -7, y = -4$ and $x = 7\frac{2}{5}, y = 3\frac{1}{5}$. The line $x - 2y = 1$ intersects the circle $x^2 + y^2 = 65$ at two points, $(-7, -4)$ and $(7\frac{2}{5}, 3\frac{1}{5})$.

3 (2, 3)

Exercise 1E

1 (a) $x = -3, y = 1$ and $x = 4, y = 8$

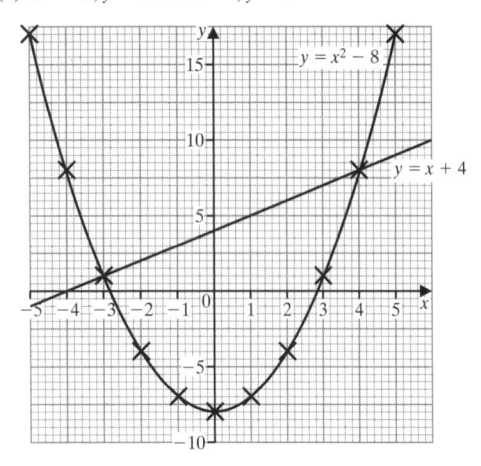

(b) $x = -5, y = 27$ and $x = 1, y = 3$

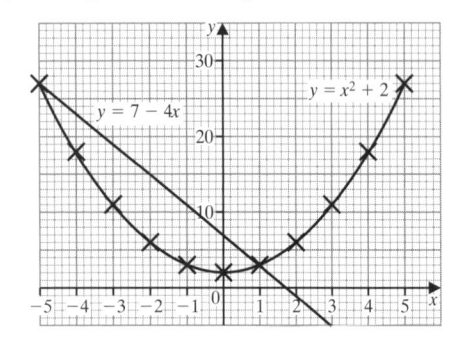

(c) $x = -4, y = -13$ and $x = 2, y = -1$

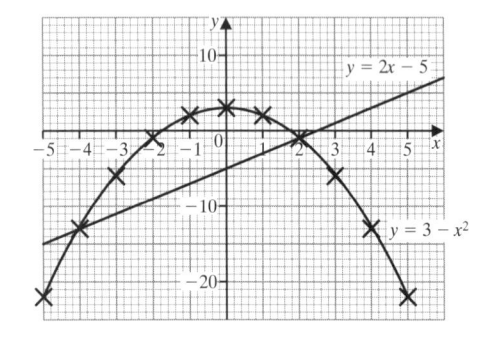

(d) $x = -3, y = 5$ and $x = -1, y = 3$

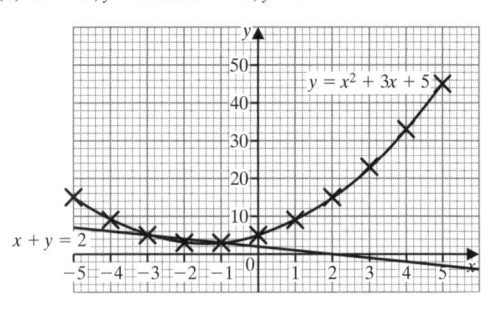

2 (a) $x = -3, y = -4$ and $x = 4, y = 3$

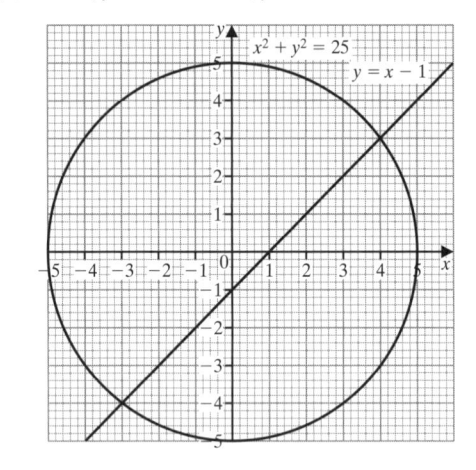

(b) $x = -8, y = -6$ and $x = 6, y = 8$

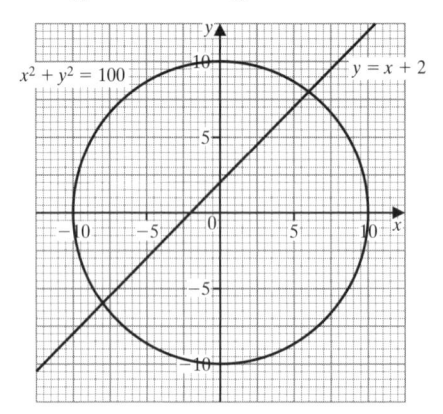

Answers 97

(c) $x = 0, y = 5$ and $x = 3, y = 4$

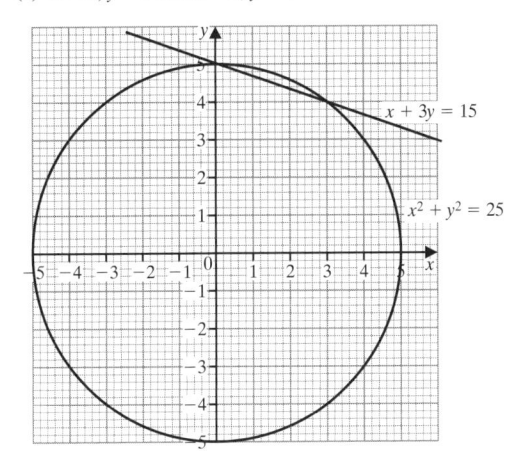

(d) $x = -8, y = 6$ and $x = 6, y = -8$

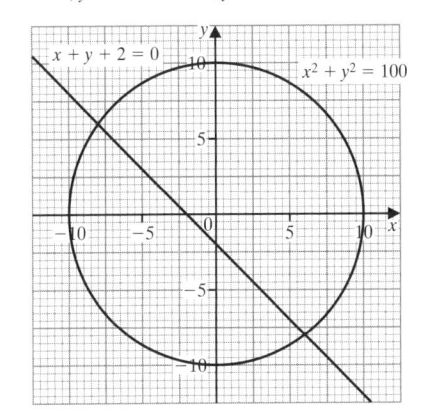

3 (a) $x = -2, y = -2$ and $x = 5, y = 19$
   (b) $x = -6, y = 13$ and $x = 1, y = -1$
   (c) $x = -2, y = 1$ and $x = 3, y = 11$
   (d) $x = -5, y = 27$ and $x = 1, y = 3$
   (e) $x = -3, y = -1$ and $x = -1, y = 3$
   (f) $x = -3, y = 7$ and $x = 7, y = -3$
   (g) $x = -4\frac{2}{5}, y = -\frac{4}{5}$ and $x = 4, y = 2$
   (h) $x = -3, y = -8$ and $x = 8, y = 3$
4 (a) $x = -\frac{2}{3}, y = \frac{1}{3}$ and $x = 1, y = 2$. The line $y = x + 1$ intersects the parabola $y = 3x^2 - 1$ at two points, $(-\frac{2}{3}, \frac{1}{3})$ and $(1, 2)$.
   (b) $x = 2, y = -3$. The line $4x + y = 5$ intersects the parabola $y = 1 - x^2$ at one point, $(2, -3)$. The line is a tangent to the parabola.
   (c) $x = 6, y = 2$. The line $3x + y = 20$ intersects the circle $x^2 + y^2 = 40$ at one point, $(6, 2)$. The line is a tangent to the circle.
   (d) $x = 1\frac{3}{5}, y = -3\frac{4}{5}$ and $x = 4, y = 1$. The line $y = 2x - 7$ intersects the circle $x^2 + y^2 = 17$ at two points, $(1\frac{3}{5}, -3\frac{4}{5})$ and $(4, 1)$.

5 (a) (b) (c)

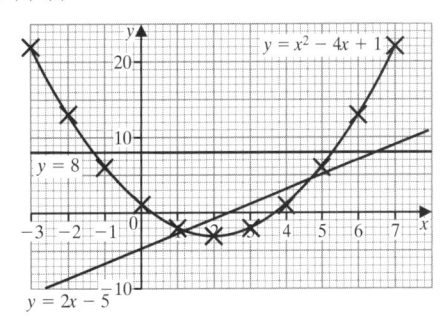

(b) $x = 5.3, x = -1.3$ (1 d.p.)
(c) $x = 4.7, x = 1.3$ (1 d.p.)
6 (a) $(4, 4)$
   (b) Solving for x gives $x^2 + (c - x)^2 = r^2$, so
   $2x^2 - 2cx + c^2 = r^2$
   Rearranging gives $2x^2 - 2cx + c^2 - r^2 = 0$
   We know the tangent only intersects the circle at one point, so there can only be one solution to the quadratic equation. This means it must factorize like $(x - a)^2 = 0$ for some a.
   So completing the square: $2x^2 - 2cx + c^2 - r^2 = 0$
   $2(x - \frac{1}{2}c)^2 - \frac{1}{2}c^2 + c^2 - r^2 = 0$
   $2(x - \frac{1}{2}c)^2 + \frac{1}{2}c^2 - r^2 = 0$
   Then, we must have $\frac{1}{2}c^2 - r^2 = 0$ or $c^2 = 2r^2$
   OR – a quicker way:
   By looking at a diagram, we see that, because of the slope of the tangent, the x- and y-coordinates of the intersection point must be the same.

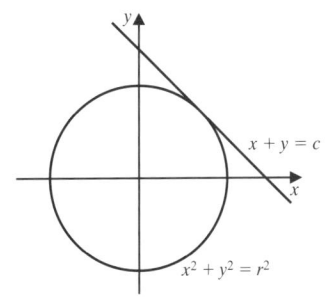

   Suppose the point is (a, a). It must satisfy both equations: $a + a = c$ and $a^2 + a^2 = r^2$.
   So, $c^2 = (2a)^2 = 4a^2 = 2 \times 2a^2 = 2r^2$.

Exercise 2A

1 (a) x^6 (b) $3x^5$ (c) $4x^2$
2 $\frac{3}{2}$
3 $3^{-10}, \sqrt[3]{3^{15}}, 27^2, 9^4$
4 (a) 5 (b) 216 (c) $\frac{1}{8}$
5 (a) x^8 (b) y^4 (c) $4w^2$
6 (a) $81x^4y^{12}$ (b) $\frac{5}{4}$ (c) 3
7 (a) $x = -1$ (b) $\frac{25}{3}x^5y^2$
8 (a) $\frac{1}{25}$ (b) 4 (c) $\frac{1}{7}$

Exercise 2B

1 $x = -4 + 2\sqrt{7}$ or $x = -4 - 2\sqrt{7}$
2 (a) $\frac{\sqrt{5}}{5}$ (b) $\frac{2\sqrt{3}}{3}$ (c) $2\sqrt{7}$ (d) $4\sqrt{5}$
3 (a) $19 + 8\sqrt{3}$ (b) 23 (c) $54 - 14\sqrt{5}$
4 (a) (i) $m = \frac{7}{2}$ (ii) $n = 1$
   (b) $t = 3$
5 $\dfrac{67 - 42\sqrt{2}}{7}$
6 $x = \pm 6\sqrt{2}$

98 Answers

7 $4 + 2\sqrt{3}$
8 $x^2 = 20$

Exercise 2C

1 $y = 5\sqrt{x}$
2 $y = \frac{30}{x}$
3 (a) $y = \frac{48}{x^2}$ (b) $y = \frac{48}{25}$ or $1\frac{23}{25}$ (c) $x = \pm 2$
4 (a) $y = \frac{25}{3}$ or $8\frac{1}{3}$ (b) $x = \pm\sqrt{24}$, i.e. $\pm 2\sqrt{6}$
5

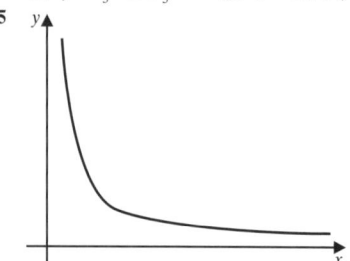

6 (a) $y = 5x^3$ (b) $y = 135$
7 $y \propto \frac{1}{x}$ so $y = \frac{k}{x}$. $y = 3$ when $x = 2$ so $3 = \frac{k}{2}$ or $k = 6$
Therefore, $y = \frac{6}{x}$ or $xy = 6$.
8 $y = 25$
9 25
10 (a) $s = 3$ (b) $t = \sqrt{3}$
11 £90
12 (a) 500 g   (b) 10 cm

Exercise 2D

1 3.655 55 (or better)
2 41.2 (1 d.p.)
3 (a) £360   (b) £288.26 (nearest penny)
4 £222 797.15 (nearest penny)
5 2.6 (1 d.p.)
6 1.77 (3 s.f.)
7 £2877.08 (nearest penny)

Exercise 2E

1 (a) x^9 (b) x^2 (c) $9n^2$
    (d) $16p^4q^2$ (e) m^2 (f) y^{-4} or $\frac{1}{y^4}$
2 (a) 5   (b) $\frac{1}{10}$ (c) $\frac{1}{4}$
3 $x = 3$
4 (a) 1   (b) $\frac{1}{6}$ (c) $\frac{3}{4}$
5 $(9\frac{1}{2})^4$, 3^5, 27^2, 9^4
6 (a) $\frac{\sqrt{13}}{13}$ (b) $7\sqrt{6}$
7 $9 + 4\sqrt{5}$
8 $x = 3 \pm 2\sqrt{6}$
9 (a) $y = 135$ (b) $\frac{1}{2}$
10 0.035 025 (or better)

Exercise 3A

1 $\frac{1}{3}$
2 $y = -\frac{1}{2}x + 5$
3 (a) (i) 3   (ii) $-\frac{1}{3}$
   (b) (i) 1   (ii) -1
   (c) (i) $\frac{1}{2}$ (ii) -2
   (d) (i) $-\frac{3}{2}$ (ii) $\frac{2}{3}$
   (e) (i) $\frac{2}{5}$ (ii) $-\frac{5}{2}$
4 (a) $y = 3x - 3$ (b) $y = -\frac{1}{3}x - 2$
5 (a) (i) $-\frac{3}{5}$ (ii) $(0, 3)$

    (b) $5y + 3x = -20$
    (c) $y = \frac{5x}{3} - 21$
6 $y = \frac{x}{5} - 3$

Exercise 3B

1 (a)

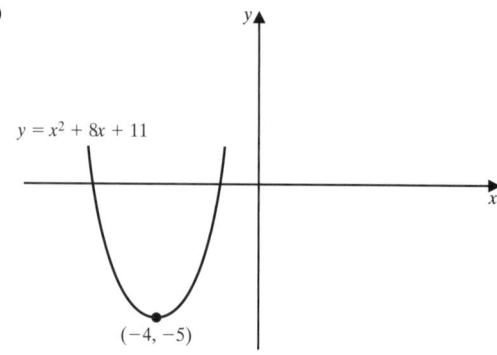

(b) Minimum value of $y = -5$, value of x at this minimum $= -4$.
2 (a) (b) (c)

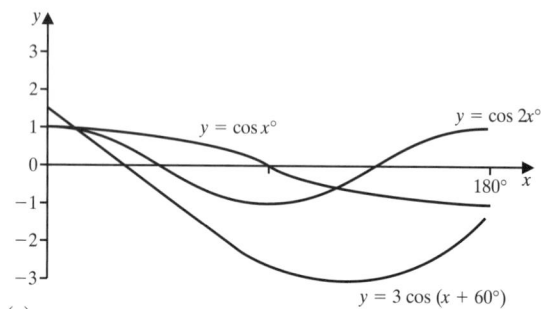

3 (a)

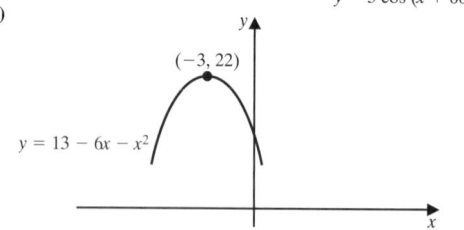

(b) Maximum value $= 22$
(c) $g(x) = -x^2 + 10x - 3$
4 (a) $(2, 5)$ (b) $(6, 5)$ (c) $(3, 7)$
   (d) $(-3, 5)$ (e) $(1\frac{1}{2}, 5)$
5 (a) (i) $A = (90, 1)$ (ii) $B = (270, -1)$
(b)

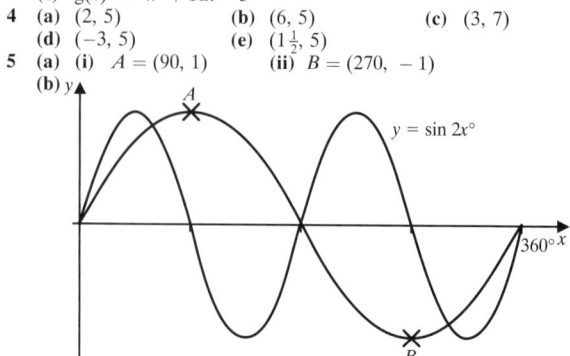

6 (a)

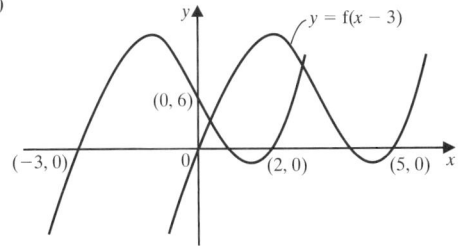

Diagram A

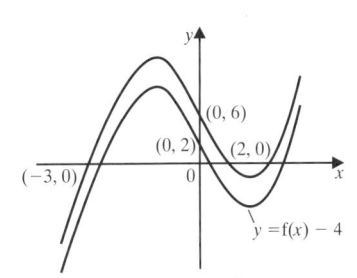

Graph showing $y = f(x-3)$ with points $(-3, 0)$, $(0, 6)$, $(2, 0)$, $(5, 0)$.

Diagram B

Graph showing $y = f(x) - 4$ with points $(-3, 0)$, $(0, 2)$, $(0, 6)$, $(2, 0)$.

Exercise 3C

1 $y = 3x$
2 (a) [graph]
   (b) 6   (c) $x = 4$
3 (a) $(2, 7)$ (b) $(-1, 4)$ (c) $(1, 4)$ (d) $(2, 8)$

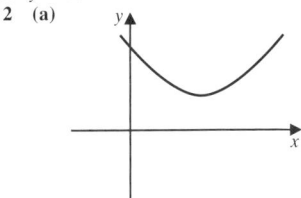

Exercise 4A

1 $a = 26.39$ (to 2 d.p.)
2 $b = 20.63$ (to 2 d.p.)
3 $c = 13.67$ (to 2 d.p.)
4 $d = 104.77$ (to 2 d.p.)
5 $e = 14.86$ (to 2 d.p.)
6 $A = 15.8°$ (to 1 d.p.)
7 $B = 52.6°$ (to 1 d.p.)
8 $C = 47.8°$ or $132.2°$ (to 1 d.p.)

Exercise 4B

(Lengths to 2 d.p., Angles to 1 d.p.)
1 $BC = 20.22$, angle $B = 40.0°$, angle $C = 20.0°$
2 $DE = 2.80$, angle $D = 123.0°$, angle $E = 34.0°$
3 $PR = 13.06$, angle $P = 98.6°$, angle $R = 47.4°$
4 $JL = 13.18$, angle $J = 38.6°$, angle $L = 24.4°$
5 $ST = 11.69$, angle $S = 21.4°$, angle $T = 15.6°$
6 $YZ = 2.57$, angle $Y = 137.9°$, angle $Z = 30.8°$

Exercise 4C

1 angle $A = 89.0°$, angle $B = 61.0°$, angle $C = 30.0°$ (to 1 d.p.)
2 angle $D = 56.3°$, angle $E = 93.8°$, angle $F = 29.9°$ (to 1 d.p.)
3 angle $J = 125.1°$, angle $K = 30.8°$, angle $L = 24.1°$ (to 1 d.p.)
4 angle $P = 25.9°$, angle $Q = 149.6°$, angle $R = 123.8°$ (to 1 d.p.)

5 (a) $AC = 9.86$ cm (3 s.f.)
   (b) Area of $ABC = 13.3$ cm^2 (3 s.f.)
   (c) Area of $ABCD = 40.0$ cm^2 (3 s.f.)
6 (a) 11.7 cm
   (b) angle $ABC = 42.5°$
7 Distance from starting point $= 462$ km (3 s.f.)
   Bearing of $064.9°$ (3 s.f.)
8 (a) Average speed $= 15.4$ km/h (3 s.f.)
   (b) $LM = 20.8$ km (3 s.f.)

Exercise 4D

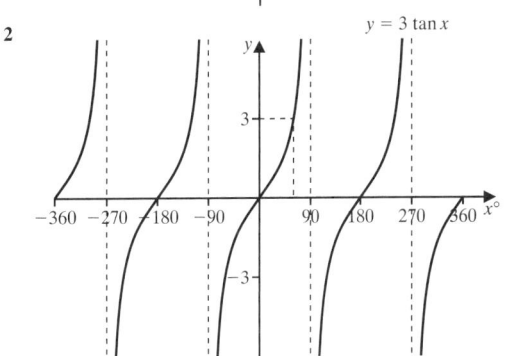

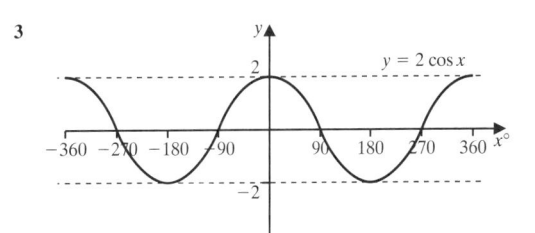

1 Graph of $y = 4 \sin x$

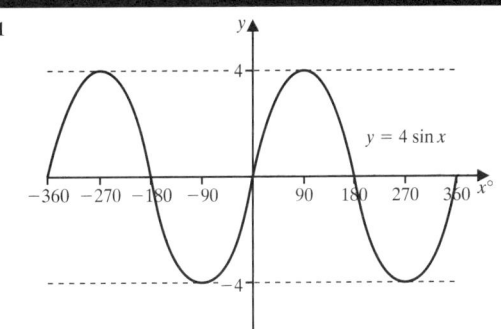

2 Graph of $y = 3 \tan x$

3 Graph of $y = 2 \cos x$

4 Graph of $y = -2 \sin x$

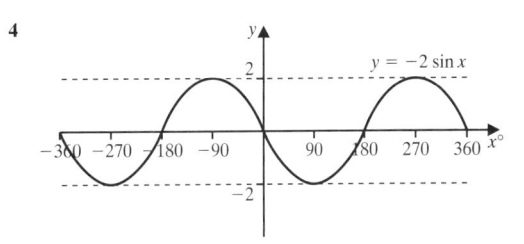

100 Answers

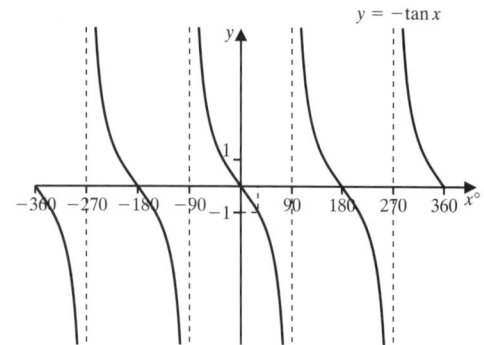

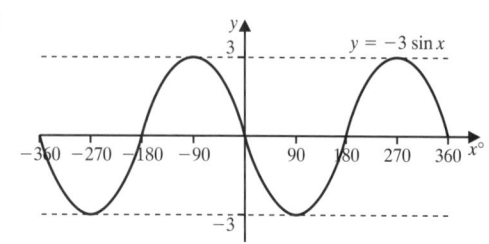

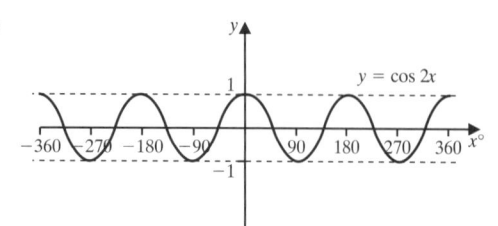

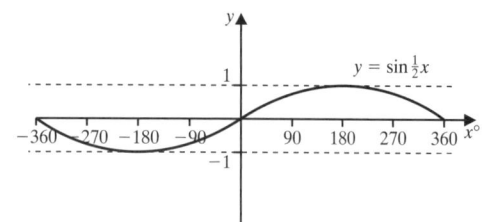

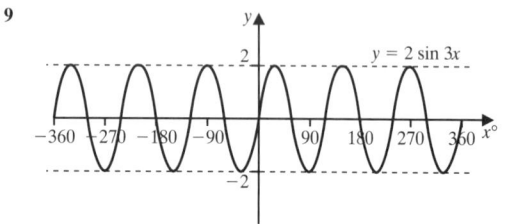

5 [Graph: $y = -\tan x$ from -360 to 360]

6 [Graph: $y = -3\sin x$ from -360 to 360]

7 [Graph: $y = \cos 2x$ from -360 to 360]

8 [Graph: $y = \sin \tfrac{1}{2} x$ from -360 to 360]

9 [Graph: $y = 2\sin 3x$ from -360 to 360]

10 [Graph: $y = 5\cos 2x$ from -360 to 360]

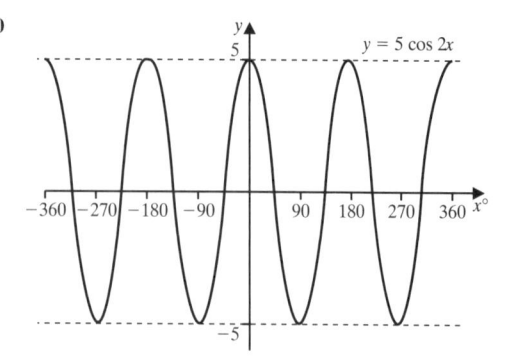

Exercise 4E

1 $x = 14.5°, 165.5°$ (1 d.p.)
2 $x = 56.3°, 236.3°$ (1 d.p.)
3 $x = 30°, 150°, 210°, 330°$
4 $x = 33.2°, 146.8°$ (1 d.p.)
5 $x = 26.2°, 86.2°, 146.2°, 206.2°, 266.2°, 326.2°, 386.2°, 446.2°, 506.2°, 566.2°, 626.2°, 686.2°$ (1 d.p.)
6 $x = -160.5°, -19.5°$ (1 d.p.)
7 $x = -84.2°, -5.8°, 95.8°, 174.2°$ (1 d.p.)
8 $x = -118.2°, -28.2°, 61.8°, 151.8°$ (1 d.p.)

Exercise 4F

1 $4.6°$ (1 d.p.)
2 $71.7°$ (1 d.p.)
3 $7.1°$ (1 d.p.)

Exercise 4G

1 $41.6°$ (1 d.p.)
2 11.1 cm (3 s.f.)
3 (a) 23.9 cm² (3 s.f.)   (b) $78.4°$ (1 d.p.)
4 69.4 m (3 s.f.)
5 243 m (3 s.f.)
6 (a) 15 feet   (b) 35 feet   (c) 6 hours
7 (a) [Graph of d (metres) vs t (hours)]
   (b) 3, 15
8 (a) $A = (90°, 0), B = (0°, 1)$
   (b) [Graph of $y = f(2x)$]

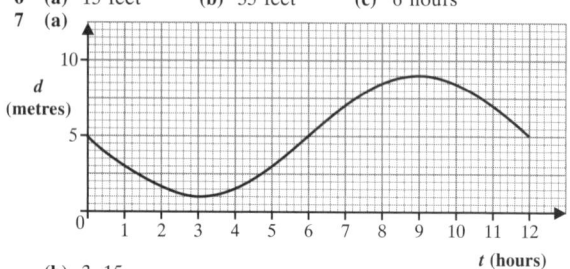

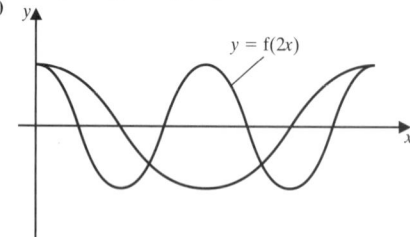

Exercise 5A

1 $a = 57°, b = 57°$
2 $c = 44°, d = 88°$
3 $e = 65°$
4 $f = 22°$
5 $g = 25°$
6 $h = 37°, i = 37°$
7 $j = 66°$
8 $k = 56°, m = 56°$

Exercise 5B

1 $a = 108°, b = 85°$
2 angle $B = 76°$
3 angle $XTY = 117°$
4 angle $TYS = 112.5°$
5 angle $ABC = 124°$
6 angle $ADC = 75°$, angle $ACD = 63°$
7 angle $ABC = 56°$, angle $BAC = 34°$

8 (a) Angle $OCE = 90°$ (tangent at right angles to radius)
       Angle $EOC = 180° - 90° - 36° = 54°$ (angles in a triangle)
       Angle $ABC = \frac{1}{2} \times 54° = 27°$ (angle at centre = 2 × angle at circumference)
   (b) Angle $ADC = 180° - 27° = 153°$ (opposite angles in a cyclic quadrilateral)

Exercise 5C

1 angle $TBA = 42°$
2 angle $ABT = 56°$, angle $BTC = 46°$
3 angle $ABT = 73°$
4 angle $BTA = 60°$
5 angle $CBT = 37°$
6 (a) $40°$
   (b) $12°$
   (c) Angle $EAD =$ angle $BAC + 38° = 78°$. If a circle could be drawn as described then angle EAD would have to be an angle in a semicircle i.e. $90°$.

Exercise 5D

1 Angle $AXB =$ angle CXD (opposite angles).
   Angle $ABX =$ angle CDX and angle $BAX =$ angle DCX (angles in the same segment). So, BXA and CXD have the same angles so are similar.
2 Angle $BAX =$ angle DCX (angle in the same segment)
   angle $BAX =$ angle CDX (alternate angles)
   So, angle $DCX =$ angle CDX and triangle CXD is isosceles.
3 angle $ATP =$ angle PBT (alternate segment theorem)
   angle $BTQ =$ angle BAT (alternate segment theorem)
   So, angle $BTP = 180° -$ angle $BTQ = 180° -$ angle $BAT =$ angle PAT
   Angle P is common to both triangles.
   So, triangles PAT and PTB have the same angles and so are similar.
4 Angle $APT =$ angle ATP (triangle PAT is isosceles)
   angle $ATP =$ angle AXT (alternate segment theorem)
   So, angle $APT =$ angle AXT and so triangle PTX is isosceles.
   So, $PT = TX$.
5 Angle $QRS = 180° -$ angle QPS (opposite angles in a cyclic quadrilateral)
   So, angle $APS = 180° -$ angle $QPS =$ angle QRS
   angle $PQR = 180° -$ angle PSR (opposite angles in a cyclic quadrilateral)
   So, angle $ASP = 180° -$ angle $PSR =$ angle PQR
   Angle A is common to both triangles.
   So, triangles APS and AQR have the same angles and so are similar.
6 Angle $APR =$ angle ABP (alternate segment theorem for smaller circle)
   angle $XPR =$ angle XYP (alternate segment theorem for larger circle)
   So, angle $XYP =$ angle $XPR =$ angle $APR =$ angle ABP
   But PY is a straight line, so AB and XY are parallel.
7 Angle $OTR = 90°$, angle $OSR = 90°$ (tangent and radius perpendicular)
   angle $TXY = 90°$ (angle in a semicircle)
   So, angle $OTR =$ angle TXY
   angle $SRT = 360° -$ angle $OTR -$ angle $OSR -$ angle SOT (angles in a quadrilateral)
   $= 180° -$ angle SOT
   angle $OYX =$ angle SOY (alternate angles)
   so angle $SRT = 180° -$ angle $SOT =$ angle SOY
   angle $XTY = 180° -$ angle $TXY -$ angle TYX (angles in a triangle)
   $= 90° -$ angle TYX
   But, angle $OQS = 180° -$ angle $OSQ -$ angle SOQ (angles in a triangle)
   $= 90° -$ angle SOQ
   So angle $OQS = 90° -$ angle $SOQ = 90° -$ angle $TYX =$ angle XTY
   So, triangles TXY and TRQ have the same angles and so are similar.
   Now, since angle $QTX =$ angle RQT we must have TX and RQ parallel.

Exercise 6A

1 (a) Volume; $\frac{4}{3}$ and π are numbers so are dimensionless, r is a length so r^3 has dimension 3. So $\frac{4}{3}\pi r^3$ has dimension 3, this represents a volume.
   (b) Volume; π is a number so is dimensionless, r is a length so r^2 has dimension 2. h is a length so h has dimension 1. So $\pi r^2 h$ has dimension 3.
   (c) Length; π is a number so is dimensionless, h is a length so h has dimension 1. So πh has dimension 1.
   (d) Area; $\frac{1}{2}$ is a number so is dimensionless, a and b are lengths so $a + b$ has dimension 1. h is a length so h has dimension 1. So $\frac{1}{2}(a + b)h$ has dimension 2.
   (e) Length; 2 is a number so is dimensionless, l and w lengths so l has dimension 1 and w has dimension 1. So $2l$ has dimension 1, $2w$ has dimension 1 and $2l + 2w$ has dimension 1.
   (f) Area; π is a number so is dimensionless, r is a length so r has dimension 1. l is a length so l has dimension 1. So $\pi r l$ has dimension 2.
   (g) Area; π is a number so is dimensionless, while r, h, d and l each have dimension 1. So the top of the fraction has dimension 3; divided by the bottom (dimension 1) this gives an expression with dimension 2.
   (h) Length; π and 2 are dimensionless, while r is a length so $\pi r^2 + 2r^2$ has dimension 2; divided by r (dimension 1) this gives an expression with dimension 1.
2 (a) Area; λ is dimensionless. x and y both have dimension 1. So λxy has dimension 2.
   (b) Volume; λ is dimensionless. x, y and z all have dimension 1. So λxyz has dimension 3.
   (c) Area; λ is dimensionless. y^2 has dimension 2. So λy^2 has dimension 2.
   (d) Area; λ^2 is dimensionless. x^2 has dimension 2. So $\lambda^2 x^2$ has dimension 2.
   (e) Length; λ is dimensionless. x, y and z all have dimension 1, so $x + y + z$ has dimension 1. So $\lambda(x + y + z)$ has dimension 1.

Exercise 6B

1 17.03 cm (to 2 d.p.)
2 $\sqrt{p^2 + q^2 + r^2}$ cm
3 (a) 22.36 cm (2 d.p.)
   (b) 22.91 cm (to 2 d.p.)
4 (a) $AC = 8.49$ cm (2 d.p.)
   (b) $AV = 15.59$ cm (to 2 d.p.)
5 (a) $EB = 21.54$ cm (to 2 d.p.)
   (b) $EC = 33$ cm

Exercise 6C

1 (a) (i) 0.979 cm^2 (ii) $3.125\pi - \frac{25}{2} \sin 45° \text{ cm}^2$
   (b) (i) 28.5 cm^2 (ii) $25\pi - 50 \text{ cm}^2$
   (c) (i) 138 cm^2 (ii) $75\pi - \frac{225}{2} \sin 120° \text{ cm}^2$
   (d) (i) 2.26 m^2 (ii) $\frac{75}{18}\pi - \frac{25}{2} \sin 60° \text{ m}^2$
2 49.7 m^2

Exercise 6D

1 15.87 cm
2 (a) 1105.92 cm^3 (b) 144 cm^2

102 Answers

3

Measurement	Aeroplane	Model of aeroplane
Area of roundel	3 m²	12 cm²
Number of wheels	4	4
Width	3.25 m	6.5 cm
Volume of cabin	200 m³	1600 cm³

4 (a) 4:25   (b) 8:125
5 216 000:1

Exercise 6E

1 (a) (i) 2400 cm³ (3 s.f.)   (ii) $\frac{2290}{3}\pi$ cm²
  (b) 796 cm³
  (c) 135 cm³ (3 s.f.)
  (d) 1700 cm³ (3 s.f.)
2 654.50 cm³ (2 d.p.)
3 $458\frac{1}{3}$ m³
4 1520.00 cm³ (2 d.p.)

Exercise 6F

1 (a) 8.38 cm (3 s.f.)
  (b) 8.13 cm (3 s.f.)
  (c) 4.73 cm² (3 s.f.)
2 Volume; λ is dimensionless and a and h each have dimension 1. h^2 has dimension 2 so λah^2 has dimension 3.
3 (a) 9:49
  (b) 27:343
4 2666π cm³
5 (a) 22.4 cm (1 d.p.)
  (b) 15.6 cm (1 d.p.)
  (c) 133° (3 s.f.)
6 (a) 12.7 cm (1 d.p.)
  (b) 13.6 cm (1 d.p.)
  (c) 64.9° (1 d.p.)
  (d) 50.2° (1 d.p.)

Exercise 7A

1 (a) Number a list of students from 1 to 1200. Use a calculator to find Ran # × 1200, and then round. Select the student with this number from the list. Repeat until 30 students have been selected.
  (b) Number a list of students from 1 to 1200. Use a calculator to find Ran # × 25, and then round. Then, starting with the student with this number, go through the list and select every 25th student.
     For example, if the random number was 3, take the 3rd, 28th, 53rd, ..., all the way to the 1178th student.
2 (a) 8 caravans
  (b) 12 caravans
3 (a) (b) Students' own answers
4 Firstly, number the adverts on each page. Use a calculator to find Ran # × 250, and then round. Turn to the page with this number. Use a calculator to find Ran # × 50, and then round. Select the advert with this number on the relevant page. Repeat the whole process until 80 adverts have been selected.
5 (a) 5 boys in Year 10.
  (b) 41 Key Stage 3 students.
6 Use a calculator to find Ran # × 50, and round. Take the name which is this number from the start of the list, and then select every 50th name from the telephone directory. For example, if the random number was 37, take 37th, 87th, 137th, ... etc., name from the telephone directory.

Exercise 7B

1 (a)

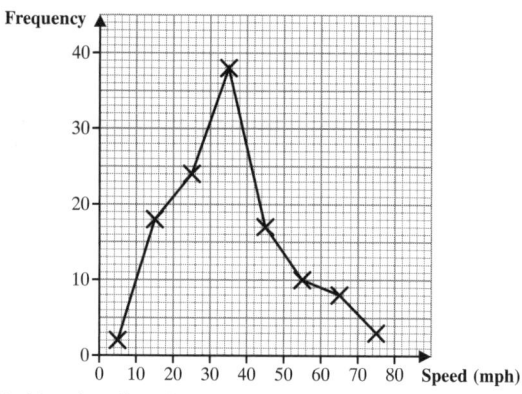

(b) 30 mph – 40 mph   (c) 35.6 mph (1 d.p.)
(d)

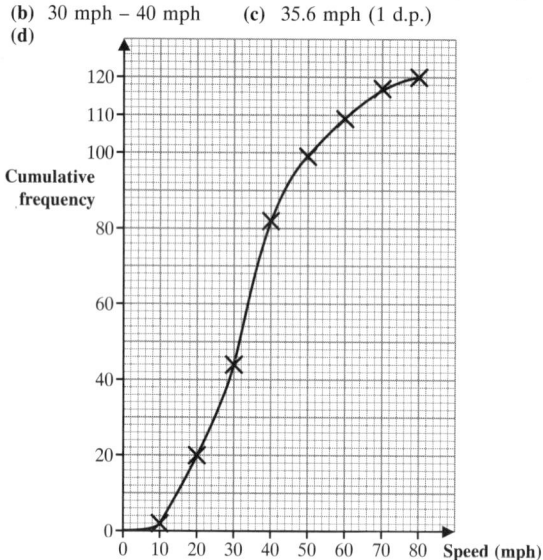

(e) (i) 34 mph
    (ii) 19 mph
    (iii) 16 cars
(f)

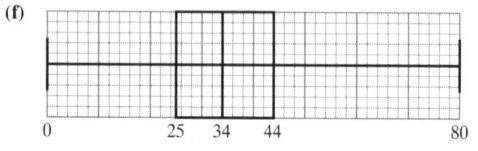

2 (a)

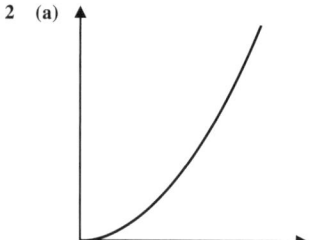

Answers 103

(b) [graph: S-shaped curve]

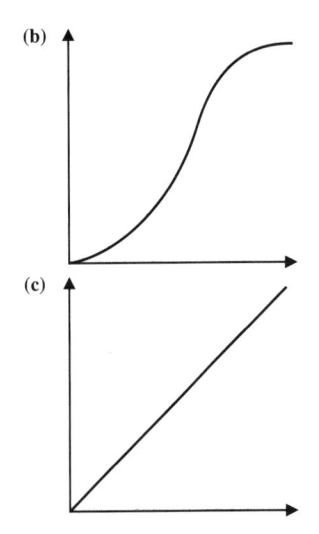

(c) [graph: straight line through origin]

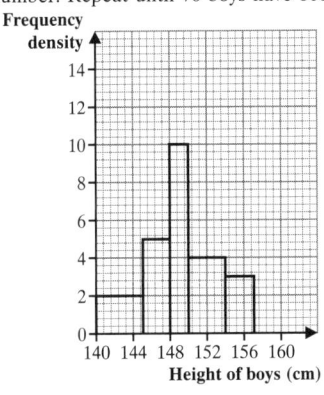

(c)
Heights of girls h centimetres	Frequency
$140 \leq h < 146$	6
$146 \leq h < 150$	8
$150 \leq h < 151$	12
$151 \leq h < 152$	13
$152 \leq h < 155$	21
$155 \leq h < 160$	10

(d) The range of the boys' heights is less than the range of the girls' heights.
The modal class interval for the boys' height (148–150 cm) is less than the modal class interval for the girls' height (151–152 cm).

3 [histogram: Frequency density vs Weight (kg)]

Exercise 7C

1 (a)
Age (a) years	Frequency
$0 < a \leq 15$	20
$15 < a \leq 20$	16
$20 < a \leq 30$	42
$30 < a \leq 40$	49
$40 < a \leq 65$	57
$65 < a \leq 70$	24
$70 < a \leq 90$	18

(b) [histogram: Frequency density vs Age (years)]

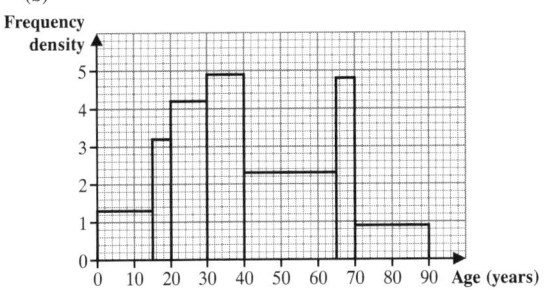

(c) 226 people
(d) 70 people; assuming that the 20–30 interval is split evenly, i.e., 21 people are aged between 20 and 25, and 21 people are aged between 25 and 30.

2 (a) Firstly, number the boys. Use a calculator to find Ran # × (total number of boys), and round. Select the boy with this number. Repeat until 70 boys have been selected.

(b) [histogram: Frequency density vs Height of boys (cm)]

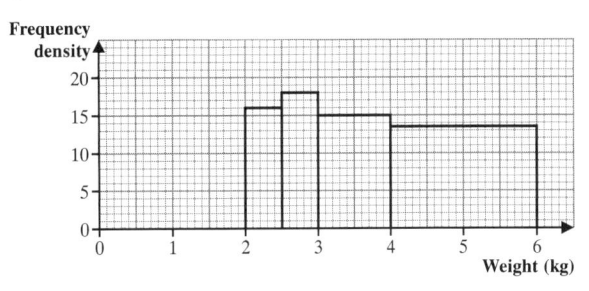

Exercise 7D

1 (a) [tree diagram: Tennis / Snooker branches with Sarah 0.3 → Sarah 0.2, Louise 0.8; Louise 0.7 → Sarah 0.2, Louise 0.8]

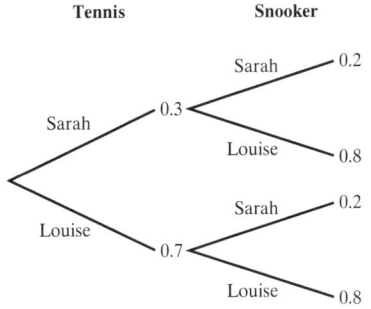

(b) (i) 0.06   (ii) 0.94
(c) 24 times

2 (a) 0.97
(b) 18 000 batteries
(c) 0.000 027; the events: '1st battery faulty', '2nd battery faulty', 3rd battery faulty' are independent, so P(all 3 batteries faulty) = P(1st faulty) × P(2nd faulty) × P(3rd faulty) = 0.03 × 0.03 × 0.03

104 Answers

Exercise 7E

1. (a) 0.9997 (b) 3600
2. Students' own answers
3. (a) 47.3 mph
   (b) [frequency polygon graph]
   (c)

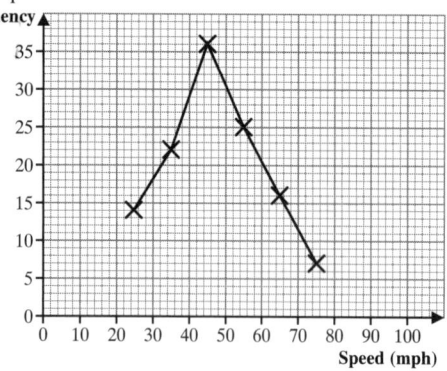

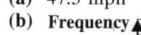

	Cumulative frequency
Up to 30 mph	14
Up to 40 mph	36
Up to 50 mph	72
Up to 60 mph	97
Up to 70 mph	113
Up to 80 mph	120

   (d) [cumulative frequency curve]
   (e) 47 (approx.) (f) (i) 38 (ii) 57 (iii) 19
   (g) [box plot: 20, 38, 47, 57, 80]

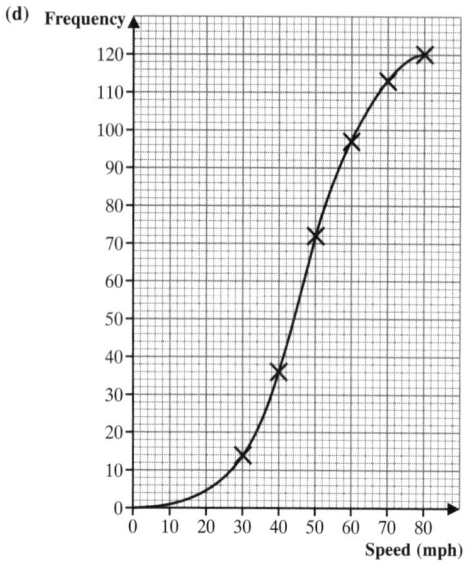

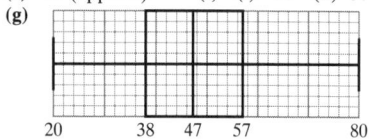

4.

Speed (s) mph	Frequency
$0 < s \leq 30$	30
$30 < s \leq 40$	40
$40 < s \leq 50$	60
$50 < s \leq 60$	30
$60 < s \leq 80$	40
$80 < s \leq 100$	10

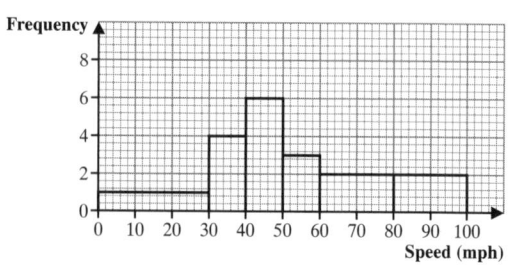

[histogram]

5. (a) 0.14 (b) 0.76
6. [blank grid of 6 squares]

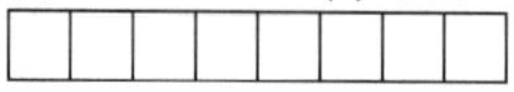

Terminal practice paper 1

1. 35 years and 28 years
2. (a) (i) x^{21} (ii) $25y^8$
   (b) $6(t - 2)$
3. (a) (b) [graph showing triangles P, Q, R]
   (c) Reflection in the line $y = x + 2$
4. (a) 7
   (b) $E = \frac{1}{2}mv^2$
5. (a) [tree diagram: A, B, C each branching to D, E, F, G]

   (b) A & D, A & E, A & F, A & G, B & D, B & E, B & F, B & G, C & D, C & E, C & F, C & G

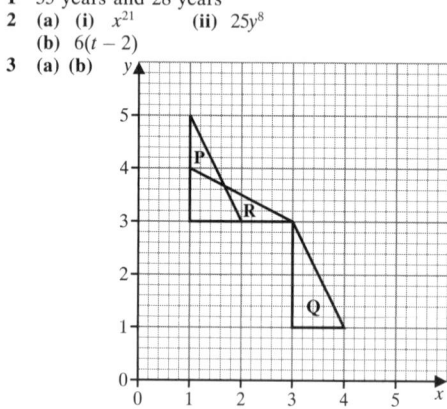

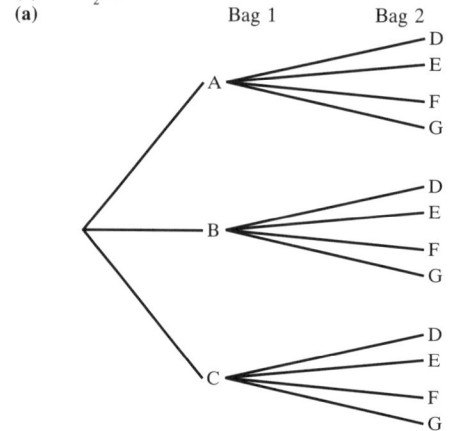

(c) 35 outcomes
(d) The outcome of the choice from the first bag does not affect the outcome of the choice from the second bag.

6 (a) $\frac{9\pi}{2}$ cm²   (b) $(6+3\pi)$ cm
7 (a) 2   (b) 125   (c) $\frac{1}{4}$
8 (a) $y = 5x^2$ (b) $y = 45$
9 (a) $4\sqrt{5}$ (b) $9 - 4\sqrt{5}$
10 Angle $ABC = 48°$. Angle $ACB = 48°$, by the alternate segment theorem, and angle $ABC = $ angle ACB since triangle ABC is isosceles.
11

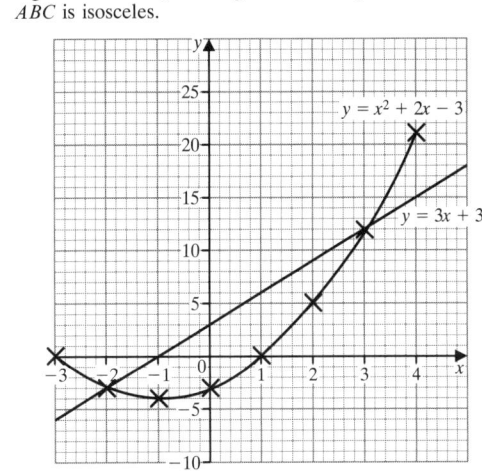

$x = -2$ and $x = 3$

12 (a) $x = 15$
   (b) Disagree. Since 31 lies within a class interval it is impossible to say exactly how many candidates got 31 or more.
   We can estimate, by assuming the 30–35 class is evenly spread so that the number of candidates getting 31 or more and less than 35 is 80, but this gives an estimate of $80 + 140 + 50 = 270$ which is more than half the number of candidates.
13 $x = -\frac{3}{5}, y = 4\frac{1}{5}$ and $x = 3, y = -3$
14 (a)

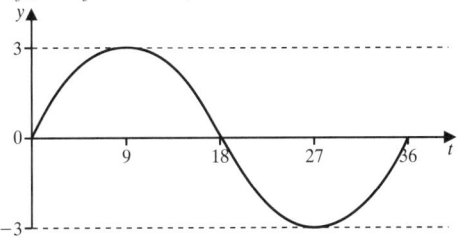

(b) The graph $y = 3\sin 10t$ intersects the line $y = 1$ in two places in the range $0 \leqslant t \leqslant 36$, so there are two solutions to $3\sin 10t = 1$ in the range $0 \leqslant t \leqslant 36$.

Terminal practice paper 2

1 (a) 1.93207951956
   Note: some calculators have room for fewer digits e.g. an 8-digit calculator would show 1.9320795. Also, the calculator may round the number incorrectly, so allow a tolerance of 1 in the last given digit.
   (b) 1.93
2 $x = 35$
3 460.53 g
4 (i) E   (ii) C   (iii) B   (iv) A   (v) D
5 £635

6

7 angle $ACB = 53°$
8 (a) $y = 2x - 7$
   (b) $y = -\frac{1}{2}x + 3$
9 (a) 8.70 m/s (to 3 s.f.)
   (b) 9 m/s. The average speed is between 8.54 m/s and 8.70 m/s, but these are different to 2 s.f. so the appropriate degree of accuracy is 1 s.f.
10 (a) $3(x-5)(x+5)$
   (b) $\dfrac{3(x+5)}{4x+3}$
11 5.35 cm² (to 3 s.f.)
12 (a)

Age (years)	Number in sample
16	12
17	27
18	21

   (b) 515 female students
13 (a) $MV = 6.78$ cm (to 3 s.f.)
   (b) angle $= 58.0°$ (to 1 d.p.)
14 (a) $(x-2)^2 - 4$
   (b) (i)

   (ii)

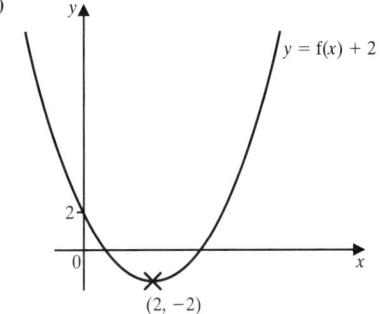

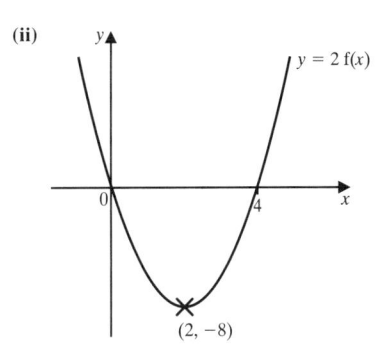